OFF THE FRONT FOOT

OFF THE FRONT FOOT

HOW TO STAY ONE STEP AHEAD IN LIFE
MARK INGLIS

REVIEW COPY
NZ Retail: $34.95
N.Z. Pub Date:
IMPRINT: 17 Oct 2003
RANDOM HOUSE N.Z. LIMITED
Phone (09) 444 7197 Fax (09) 444 7580

RANDOM HOUSE
NEW ZEALAND

National Library of New Zealand Cataloguing-in-Publication Data

Inglis, Mark, 1959-
Off the front foot : how to stay one step ahead in life / Mark Inglis.
ISBN 1-86941-570-1
1. Self-help techniques. 2. Goal (Psychology). 3. Motivation
(Psychology) I. Title.
158.1—dc 21

A RANDOM HOUSE BOOK
published by
Random House New Zealand
18 Poland Road, Glenfield, Auckland, New Zealand
www.randomhouse.co.nz

First published 2003

© 2003 Mark Inglis

The moral rights of the author have been asserted

ISBN 1 86941 570 1

Design and layout: Kate Greenaway
Cover design: Katy Yiakmis
Main cover illustration: *New Zealand Herald*; smaller illustrations: Mark Inglis

Printed in Australia by Griffin Press Ltd

Contents

SECTION ONE
LESSONS THAT HAVE GIVEN ME A 'LEG UP' IN LIFE
1. Challenge: the essence of life 9
2. From stumbling blocks to stepping stones 20
3. Shedding the chains: embracing change 25
4. Must do, not can do 33
5. Dream big 39
6. Passion and commitment: the rungs in the ladder to success 44
7. No fences 51

SECTION TWO
STEPPING OVER SOME OF LIFE'S STUMBLING BLOCKS
8. Procrastination: we'll talk about it later 59
9. Learn to stand outside yourself 63
10. Some days that glass is just half empty 71
11. The terrible P word: planning 77
12. Communication: easy to say, harder to do 84
13. Frustration: learning to live with things you can't change 92

14. What to do if it all turns to custard   97
15. Balance: essential on the bike, on the
    cliff and in life   112

SECTION THREE
LESSONS TO BE LEARNED FROM SPORT
16. Race yourself: the secret to winning   123
17. In the zone, but what zone?   131
18. Visualisation: seeing it happen, making it happen   137

SECTION FOUR
MARK'S PASSIONS
19. The culture of the bike: the last hard sport?   149
20. Go high young man: what mountaineering is
    all about   163
21. You are what you eat   173

SUMMARY
22. Tying it all together: lifelong learning   185

Section One

*Lessons
that have given me
a 'leg up' in life*

1. Challenge: the essence of life

Hi, if we haven't met, I'm Mark Inglis, a double below-knee amputee Kiwi who thinks he has learned a few lessons from his experiences and would like to share some of them with you. I've recently written an autobiographical tale called *No Mean Feat*, which describes many of the passions in my life, in particular mountaineering and cycling. However, my real life story and the core lesson that I have learned from it so far is all about CHALLENGE. Over time, I have come to understand that the concept of challenge and the benefits that accrue from taking on challenge have been the key to my life up to this point and I hope they will be the key to my future. But I guess to help you understand that a bit better we need to go back — way, way back, so my kids tell me (Anne, my wife, and I are accompanied and directed through life by our three children, Amanda (13), Jeremy (18) and Lucy (21)).

WHO AM I AND WHERE AM I FROM?

I grew up in the South Island in the small South Canterbury town of Geraldine. Blessed with loving and hard-working parents (Mary and Jim) I grew up in a semi-rural environment, surrounded by people who worked hard for their living.

Dad was a farm worker, a shearer, a truck driver, and also the best — and fussiest — damn grader driver you can imagine. His roads were works of art, and it was a shame to drive on them, or at least he certainly thought so!

Mum worked throughout much of my childhood, so over the years us kids (I'm the baby of three, Anne and John are older and probably wouldn't want me to tell you by how much) became quite skilled in cooking and looking after the house and ourselves. We weren't an affluent family by any measure, but Mum and Dad always stretched the purse strings to ensure we rarely missed an opportunity, and this also taught us to fend for ourselves.

I was a bit of a runt at school, certainly the last person to be picked for team games like rugby, which was lucky really as I had a great aversion to the game. I never minded injuring myself, but could never see the sense in letting others beat you up, all over a ball that didn't even bounce properly. I was definitely a dreamer though, and then, like now, passionate about new adventures and challenges. I was introduced to mountaineering as a sport while at school in Geraldine and found in it a culture of challenge and personal responsibility that has formed the backbone of my life thus far.

As Tolkien once said: 'Not all those who wander are lost.' This book will analyse many of the challenges I've encountered during the wandering that has made up my very lucky life: from mountaineering in Mount Cook National Park in the late 1970s and early 1980s, through the 13 days near the summit of Aoraki/Mount Cook in the storm that nearly took my life, and through the understanding of disability and ability over the years, culminating in my silver medal at the Sydney 2000 Paralympics and recent ascent of the mountain that claimed my legs 20 years earlier.

RISK EVERYTHING

Risk is a concept that underlies all challenge and defines the very nature of challenge. I believe that for a challenge to be worthwhile it needs to be the hardest thing on earth for you at that time. 'The hardest thing on earth for you' is the critical part of challenge that all people need to understand. Challenge isn't just one thing and it certainly isn't the same for every individual either.

However, if you continuously face challenges, one of two things can happen, either:

1. You collapse under the strain, lose confidence in your ability and walk away defeated, perhaps to fight another day or else to drift into a life of non-challenge; or
2. You win the occasional 'impossible' and are then encouraged to have a go at the next impossible, and before long you find the impossibles have become possible.

The secret is in getting to '2' — it's in knowing how to aim high so that any win is worthwhile, but not so high as to make winning continuously unattainable, because that's '1'.

Actually, I have a bit of a head start on a lot of you in that I have grown up a mountaineer, a culture to which challenge is integral, and in that I am also a double amputee, someone for whom challenge is a daily task. I look at a target, a dream, and I know it's attainable, so the only question I ask myself is what it will take to do it and whether it is worth it. Often, others will look at me, see my disability, and then underestimate my ability and dismiss my stickability. So when I eventually succeed (not always the first time, that's for sure) I frequently find their reactions to my success somewhat over the top, so I then find myself playing down the achievement to compensate for their over-reaction. The essence here is that the achievements aren't unique to me, it's just that I have the opportunity.

I have always found it ironic that although for much of my early life I avoided team sports like the plague, it wasn't until after I was high on

Mount Cook one day, stretched to the limit and calling out, 'Hold!', meaning I was close to falling, that I realised that I was participating in the ultimate team sport. When you put your life in the hands of your team-mates, that's total personal and team commitment, expressed at its most extreme.

Thus, for me, the ultimate challenge can always be found on mountains. So many times I would be scared out of my skin, only to realise later that overcoming that fear was what it was all about, making me a stronger person incrementally every time. So how did I come to lose my legs? Well I lost them to the pursuit of challenge, the undertaking of risk.

CHALLENGE AND RISK — THE COST

In November of 1982 Phil Doole, a summer mountaineer with our search and rescue team at Mount Cook National Park, and I decided to tackle the East Ridge of Aoraki/Mount Cook as a training climb for our summer of rescuing other climbers. Phil and I hadn't climbed together before but would soon be jumping out of a helicopter in difficult conditions in our high alps, so a training climb to establish our team dynamic was required. The East Ridge of Cook is an elegant ice climb on the arête that divides the expansive East Face from the steep ice sheet that is the Caroline Face. At grade 3+, it is a serious but thrilling undertaking.

The weather the day of the climb was a building nor'west storm, but being on the sheltered lee side of the 'hill' meant we climbed into some seriously bad weather. We made the decision to try and make it over the summit ridge and down to the Empress Shelf (and safety) on the western flank of the mountain. Why? The ice conditions were difficult and the East Ridge is a very long way down, especially when tired. The risk of a fall in the dark was too great. As it turned out, the wind on the top was also too great. In fact, it was blowing so hard it was lifting us off the ice and blowing us over. What's worse, the wind kills, not just by physically blowing you off the mountain, or even because of the disorientation and distraction it causes, but through hypothermia, literally freezing you to death. Only one thing to do in that situation, and that's get out of the wind — or die.

The challenge of staying alive that day on the summit ridge of Cook is as good an object lesson on challenge as any. Want the 'must do' attitude. Then this is the place where it is essential.

Anyone familiar with the New Zealand Alps knows there is a crevasse just under the Middle Peak of Aoraki/Mount Cook called, in those days, Middle Peak Bergschrund. We knew it was there and scuttled in, terribly blown about and freezing, but alive. Once in we took stock of our situation:

- Bugger all food, which included half a packet of Shrewsbury biscuits, a small tin of peaches, some dry drink mixture and a Moro bar;
- The clothes we were climbing in (merino and polypropylene first layer, Vyella shirt, pile jacket and Gore-Tex shell), no sleeping bags or bivvy booties;
- No primus, and very little liquid left either;
- No radio or other means of contact (cell phones in 1982 needed a truck to cart them around);
- Intentions logged at Park HQ which indicated that we would be down by the next day.

All in all, not too bad a situation really; pretty normal for young fit professional mountaineers, and not too much of a problem when the weather was expected to clear in the next 24 to 48 hours. Just a short visit we thought; as soon as the wind velocity dropped enough to climb, then we would be on our way home.

As time would tell, we struck one of the longest spells of bad weather in New Zealand history. For the next 310 hours we would be sitting there, desperately trying to escape every day, being turned back by the force of the wind before we had even moved half a rope length away. Even worse, as each day moved on, our physical condition deteriorated. With minimal food and fluids, strength waned and frostbite took hold.

On the seventh day the weather cleared slightly, enough for a surveillance helicopter to spot us and drop bags of food, sleeping bags and radios. This life-saving drop enabled us to live through the agonising ordeal of the next six days before the eventual rescue.

Staying alive to be rescued was all about challenge. There was no choice. It was like a kind of final exam really — but a deadly one — pass and you live, fail and you . . .

We passed I guess, with a C minus, but still a pass. Our stay in what we dubbed 'Middle Peak Hotel' cost us what we initially thought would be just our toes and our pride, but eventually turned out to be our legs. After one month in hospital, on Christmas Eve 1982 I faced a new challenge as I was being wheeled into theatre to have the gangrenous lumps that were my feet removed. Well actually the big challenge was to develop over the next 20 years, building on the culture and career I developed as a mountaineer.

THE CHALLENGE/RISK EQUILIBRIUM

I believe we all have an in-built challenge or risk equilibrium, a bit like a children's see-saw. If life isn't dishing up enough risk, isn't presenting enough challenge, then we go out and look for more — that's why I spent so much time pushing my limits, first on motorbikes and then mountains. However, after the amputation of both lower limbs, I found that I had more than enough challenge re-entering normal life again — the prospect of adding more challenge and risk to my life took many years to come back to the fore.

From those first steps in the corridors of the Christchurch Artificial Limb Centre in early 1983 I came to realise that living with two plastic (yep, not wooden any more) legs can be likened to living in just one pair of shoes. Why? It all comes down to the sockets really, that and the concept of lifelong learning. While most attention is focused on the technology of the moving and bending parts of lower limbs, the real determinant of what you can do is the fit of the socket. It is the fit that transfers the power and gives ability. If you get a blister in that new pair of shoes/sockets, you need to put them on again if you want mobility, and you need to know how to manipulate them so they don't rub so bad in future. And just like having one pair of shoes, they are really not much use for specialist activities — in other words, school shoes are OK (although like most kids I never thought so) for going to school in, but they suck if you are trying to do ballet in them.

After the events of 1982 and the rehabilitation process, which commenced in 1983 (and continues for ever), the see-saw of risk and challenge gradually levelled out until I was once again needing to create challenge, rather than just having it presented to me each day. So I took on the challenge of returning to university to get an education, and then of using that education as a research scientist trying to understand the origin of our immune response. Even then the risk equilibrium meant I was rapidly pushing myself into disabled alpine skiing, craving the high that is experienced by overcoming fear.

I'm still learning to manage that see-saw, through my transformation from research scientist to winemaker in 1992, and even more recently in taking the lessons I have learned from such a diverse range of careers and sports into my new career as a motivator, writer and adventurer. In sport I have also sought out new challenges, such as in cycling on the international stage and once again taking on the high mountains (in this respect it seems as if my life has followed fashion — yep, I'm the living version of the revival of 'flares').

These are just a few of the challenges I have both sought out and have had to face. I always consider myself lucky in that I have both chosen and been forced into challenges; lucky because as that young mountaineer I chose risk, and came to understand the 'payback' from challenge; and lucky in being forced into challenge and change in losing my legs. That taught me new strategies to cope, many of which I'll try and pass on through this book.

TAKING THE FIRST STEP

Here's a challenge: have you ever bungy jumped? I haven't. Imagine if you will, a double amputee, bungy cord tied around their fibreglass ankles, plunging down, stretching that cord and slowing down. Just as their body weight starts to defy gravity with the help of the bungy cord, 'pop', straight out of the sockets they fly — bloody funny I'm sure, but bound to be associated with significant pain and damage. For an amputee to bungy jump they need to wear a harness just as a climber does.

Well I've fallen off enough rock faces and climbing walls in my time to mirror the feeling of the bungy jump so it has never held too much attraction, other than just to say I've done it, but every time I'd go to Auckland I'd look up at the Sky Tower and think 'challenge', think, 'I need to go to the top of that and jump off it'. Well the opportunity came recently to do just that. I was privileged to climb to the top of the Sky Tower with Olympian Dick Quax and two Special Olympic athletes, as part of an event to help raise awareness and funds for the Special Olympic movement. The climb is called Vertigo, 44 metres up vertical ladders inside the tower to the 'crow's nest', about 300 metres above the city. (A fantastic view, and definitely a buzz these days to see the tiny landing as I drive in from the airport.) But as usual the climb wasn't enough and the idea of doing the Sky Jump seemed a natural progression. To climb to the top and fly down — now there's an idea, there's a real challenge. The Sky Jump is a 192-metre wire-assisted free fall, a bit like skydiving with a hand brake.

Now for me the challenge, the risk, wasn't the height, and it wasn't even the trip down — for me the whole essence of the Sky Jump challenge can be summed up in one word: 'faith'. Faith in the professionals who tie the wire to you. It is like the ultimate big step, right out into the unknown — a step that is doubly hard for an old mountaineer like me whose skills have always focused on staying attached. What I had to do to make that jump was put my life in the hands, professionalism and skill of others. *They* put my harness on, not me; *they* tied the guide and safety rope to it, not me. The step off the Sky Tower is a huge step that first time, and the faith you must have in tackling the unknown has to be complete. It is a real step as well, rather than the bungy fall; in fact, you can run and jump it — really awesome. The guy before me 'froze' so he eventually got a helping hand (yep, they threw him off). It must have been a genuine 'learning experience' as in minutes he was back up, still scared of heights but ready to take the next leap himself, knowing that he had just shed some chains in his life and that next time it would be easier.

IDENTIFY YOUR CHALLENGES

What are your challenges? Every day is a challenge for most of us, perhaps more for some than others. Here are a few of my daily challenges and others I have faced in recent years:

- Getting up every morning and putting my legs on, especially on those days when I know it's going to hurt; that's challenge.
- Equally challenging are the days when they just slip on, feel great and I know I can get out there and step up to the next level.
- Trying to be a parent; this really is a challenge.
- Stepping away from a career as a successful winemaker; that's challenge.
- Motivating others, showing them the lessons I've learned, and am continuing to learn; that's challenge.
- Putting my hand up to be selected for the 2000 Sydney Paralympics and the subsequent training and competition; that was challenge.
- Going back to Mount Cook in 2001/2002; that was challenge.
- Not hiding my disability, in fact displaying my ability; that's challenge too.

As you can see from this brief list, challenge comes from so many elements in life, from within myself, as I race myself harder than anyone else, and just as often as a reaction to others. Challenge is risk; it is facing up to your fears. For me, mountaineering still frequently scares me, as I put myself in positions where self-doubt has the potential to kill you; as such, it is an activity that challenges you to have faith in your decision making, your skill, and frequently — and even more importantly — in the skill of others.

To me, the role of challenge in life is just like riding a bike. Let the bike free-wheel without pedalling and you will eventually go slower and slower, grinding to a halt: you will not get to go anywhere. Sure, if you are lucky you might get a bit of downhill for some speed but that sort of luck will always run out. But take that same bike and put some power into riding it, make those pedals spin, and you will get some real speed — in fact, you will go somewhere. That to me is the essence of challenge: without putting the work, the power into life, you will just get diminishing returns, you'll slow down until you stop and stagnate, you will go nowhere. Putting a challenge into your life is like putting power into those pedals — you will go somewhere.

The challenge I present to you is to find your own 'mountain to climb' — whether it be in business, in sport, or in life, put power into your life. The challenges you find and attempt will help define and enrich you and your life to an ever greater extent.

SUMMARY PANEL
Challenge

- *Challenge is the essence of life.*
- *Attempt the impossible — the hardest thing on earth for you at that time.*
- *No true challenge is without risk — or potential cost.*
- *Tip the balance of your in-built challenge/risk equilibrium.*
- *The first step is always the hardest — take it.*
- *There are no problems in this world, just challenges — define your challenges.*
- *Put some power into those pedals of life — look for challenges.*

2. From stumbling blocks to stepping stones

When one door closes, invariably another door opens, but frequently we are so busy staring at the closed door and mourning its closing that we don't see the other door. On Christmas Day 1982 I had an opportunity to experience a door closing in my life and a new one opening as I woke up to my first day as a double amputee.

OBSTACLES OR OPPORTUNITIES?
After the month of hospitalisation I had thought that I was ready for a new life, a new opportunity. Little did I know that even as the optimist that I am I had totally underestimated the effect the amputation was to have on me. When I woke from the general anaesthetic properly on Christmas Day both my body and mind felt trashed — what I had thought was going to be a bright new start in life turned out to be a bigger stumbling block than I had ever imagined.

It took me probably five days of blackness before I was able to lift my head above the murk, to free my mind of the drugs that were controlling the pain. Those drugs are a double-edged sword, in that while they dull pain they also dull down the ability to think clearly and they induce an inertia that is difficult to overcome. I can only compare it to wading painfully through uncomfortably deep and sticky mud and it is only when you can rise above it that you can focus on the future.

Nevertheless, above it I got, although it took a while. A pretty unpleasant time it was as well, not so much because of the raw pain as the discomfort and humiliation of being ill, of feeling weak and helpless.

GENERATE THE POWER TO OVERCOME

The question I'm regularly asked is how do you turn it around, how do stumbling blocks become stepping stones for some but brick walls for others? Well the motivation has to come from inside because, as you will see elsewhere in this book, you are the only one who can make up your mind to climb over that wall. Certainly others can assist, and perhaps give you some of the hints and skills that will help, but it is down to you in the end.

First and foremost you need to activate your sense of self-preservation as the base to build on. If you can then find a focus or a sense of purpose, then that is the start. From there the next step is to generate the self-belief to recognise that *everything* is possible. For myself, that came from reading of the exploits of individuals who had been there before me, stories of people who have displayed more human spirit than I'll ever come near: Sir Douglas Bader, the double-amputee fighter pilot of the Second World War and Norman Croucher, another double amputee, but a climber and adventurer. The stories of both these men in the days before and after their amputations provided me a baseline for what was possible for a double amputee — in fact, what was possible for anyone.

Outside perspectives like these certainly help during difficult times, but that confidence to go on, that confidence that you will rise above still comes from within — but don't worry, it doesn't come all at once. The thing to remember is that those bleak moments come from inside, come from your reaction to the environment, both physical and emotional (usually I have found a combination of both), in which you find yourself. Similarly, the power to turn the situation around also comes from within.

STEPPING UP

Every four years there is an event that defines the essence of transforming stumbling blocks into stepping stones, the Paralympics. The Sydney 2000 Paralympics consumed much of my life throughout 1999 and 2000.

Nothing ever changes immediately though. As we all know, everything is possible, it's just that some things take a little more time than others. That is certainly the case when recovering from an amputation, or in fact any debilitating injury. My entry back into sport certainly wasn't immediate — it took several years. In fact it is interesting to note that most Paralympians are significantly older, or at least the spread of ages is much greater, than athletes in the Olympic movement. While sport is used to help rehabilitate, to reach the elite level required for the Paralympics takes a significant commitment to training. And that training doesn't just include the usual aspects of physiology and skill, but training of the disability or condition as well. In addition, by the time you are over the initial recovery period, have got your life back on track and then have thoughts about sport, the years have slipped by.

I left New Zealand with the team in late September 2000 thinking I was just going to a big sporting event. However, I was to find that I was participating in a celebration of ability on an international scale.

To be immersed in the atmosphere was both exciting and at the same time disturbing, as I was going from being almost unique to just one of over 3500 elite disabled athletes. Every athlete there had a story like mine; in fact many had survived far more traumatic experiences and had had to work even harder to get there. If you could bottle the essence of that spirit then it would go a long way towards fixing the ills of the world in my opinion.

We got the first inkling of such an atmosphere before we left New Zealand. At the team gathering 18 hours before departure we were addressed by Sir Murray Halberg, the Olympic and world champion middle-distance runner of the 1960s and founder of the Halberg Trust. Sir Murray stood in front of us and congratulated everyone in the room for getting as far as they had, for putting in the hard work to make the Paralympic Team, indeed to be in the top echelon of our respective sports, worldwide. Every one of us was starting to preen by this stage — yep we were the best — what no one in the room expected was the next five words: 'Well that's not good enough!'

Sir Murray looked into the eye of every athlete and told us it was time to 'step up'. It was time to take the responsibility for our life and performance onto our own shoulders and perform to a level never before reached. He described what we all needed to do as being like climbing a set of stairs with a door at the top; it was our role to step up, move up those stairs and open that door. He challenged us to open that door to a new level of achievement, that of the world stage.

Every person in that room knew exactly what he meant because each of us had already done that many times, each person had already had to 'step up' in life just to be there, just to live a life. Each person had had to 'step over' those stumbling blocks that were presented to them. Every one of them had done it differently, with differing levels of expertise, but had done it nevertheless.

Sir Murray's 'step up' lesson is applicable to people in every sphere, not just a bunch of Paralympians, and its message is integral to converting those stumbling blocks into stepping stones, to achieving the mindset that you can always do better, that you have a responsibility to yourself to find a way up. You will see in the other chapters that deal with the difficult things in life the common thread of 'the choice is yours' — it is *you* who determines your thoughts. The core realisation that comes with understanding the concept of stumbling blocks and stepping stones is that the situations are one and the same — a stumbling block is exactly the same situation as a stepping stone, the only difference is in how we approach the situation.

SUMMARY PANEL
From stumbling blocks to stepping stones

- *Obstacles are just another form of opportunity.*
- *The power to overcome comes from within.*
- *Use others as a catalyst for your inspiration.*
- *Everything is possible; some things just take a bit more time.*
- *Learn to 'step up'.*

3. Shedding the chains: embracing change

If you would like to learn about change and how to get really good at it, then try going from being a young, very fit, competent climber and runner to a legless mountaineer. I can assure you there weren't too many aspiring to positions open in that career path.

IF YOU DON'T LIKE IT, CHANGE IT
The buzz word in business these days seems to be 'change management' — well that pretty well defines my life, as well as all our lives. But let's get one thing clear from the start: as a person, as Mark Inglis, let alone as a double amputee, one of my pet hates is people who moan without action. I've always believed that if you don't like something, then change it. If you don't want to change it, it surely can't be that bad, so quit moaning about it. Even if you cannot see a way to change a situation, or feel it is outside your power to do so, then the first thing you need to

do is change your attitude to the situation. Life will be very tough and a burden if you continuously moan about something, so perk up. With the right attitude you may just find yourself very surprised at how quickly the change you thought would never happen, happens.

Sure, if something isn't right, comment on it if necessary (it often feels good to have a moan), but if it affects you negatively, then you need to change either it or your reaction to it. Actually, these days I have what I call a 'moaning monitor'; it's a great tool to help me decide whether I need to implement change. All you need to do is listen to yourself. When you get home at night, how much of your conversation with your wife, partner, kids, cat, dog, or whoever, is based around moaning about your day? How much time do you spend criticising your workmates or your boss? If complaints of this nature start to dominate the conversation then it's time to change something.

DON'T RESIST CHANGE, USE IT TO GROW

Some change isn't and never will be instant and exactly as you require. Normally it will require heaps of work, but it also requires the first step. I always find it interesting that on the one hand we don't like change, but on the other we all want change. Every day we read in the papers about dog attacks, crimes of violence, the stupidity of the human race in general, especially where it affects us, and we think, 'They have got to change!' The irony is that while we often think of others as being blind to their situation and desperately want them to change, we resist with a vengeance any change directed toward us.

Change is something the wine industry in particular has had to do to survive, and still has to do to be a significant force in the world wine market. Many of the lessons I learned about my own personal change I was able to use in the 10 years that I worked as a member of a winemaking team, and equally, I learned a lot of positive and negative lessons about change and its management in the process.

When I joined the industry in February of 1992, industry share prices were low, many wine companies were very close to being on the financial rocks and I couldn't work out why. The wines were good and getting better, the people in the industry possessed a real passion and commitment to the wines, but they just weren't making enough money. In most cases the companies were frugal, no frills at all, and produced many millions of litres of wine, but the problem was it was the wrong sort of wine. The culture of the time was overly obsessed with how many litres the companies produced, rather than the profit per litre, a shift in perspective which required a subtle but important mind change.

The culture changed through the appointment of ex-winemakers to senior company positions; people like Peter Hubscher, one of the founding winemakers of the New Zealand wine industry and now the head of Montana. These were the people who were passionate about making great wine, but as efficiently as possible — a skill which requires good strategic thinking, an intimate understanding of the process, and the ability to motivate people at all levels of the industry. What people in those positions needed to do was lift the quality of the wines while keeping them affordable and concentrate on the profit per litre of each wine, not the quantity of wine or gross revenue.

This wasn't as easy as it sounds for several reasons:

- The wine-buying public had to be re-educated and convinced that the quality was there; in other words, preconceptions developed over years of consuming the cheapest wines had to be broken down and a new image created.
- The strength of the industry was its very stable workforce, yet the biggest hindrance to change was this very same stable workforce!
- Everyone had to buy into the challenge of changing the industry as wine isn't made by just one person.

These were the real hurdles and ones that required not just education or results to act as a catalyst for change, but a combination of both. Most importantly, the people who constituted the wine industry needed the commitment to instigate the change.

INITIATE AND CREATE CHANGE
Quite often the toughest part of any job is encouraging people to change, sometimes in fact demanding that people change, to survive. Usually the first reaction to change for many is to become defensive, and display anger and frustration. The lesson to learn though, is if change is really needed, then we need to take charge of the change *we* want to see, as it is we who control our thoughts — no one else should.

For instance, in any industry, change has to flow from the top to the bottom. You can't ask a wage worker to change, or to make perceived sacrifices (such as giving in or having to rethink a 15-year-old injustice or grudge with another work group), if the senior staff — generally paid significantly more — don't assume ownership and leadership of that very change. Unfortunately, that is what is seen in many cases.

As an example of change, the wine industry in New Zealand is excellent. They have handled the strategic change well, but it is a dynamic thing, constantly needing re-evaluation and ongoing commitment to change.

Personally, I've learned what some see as the 'secrets of change' because initially I was forced into it and have since come to understand that for me, change is an essential component of happiness in life, especially as it is intimately associated with challenge and opportunity.

BREAK OUT OF THE 'CAGES' OF THE PAST
Probably the hardest thing about change is letting go of the past, letting go of the problems, stresses, failures, and perhaps even successes that have gone before. Although either positively or negatively the past has shaped who you are today you must be able to let go of it if you are to make the most of the future.

Sure, you may have learned heaps, and I hate the concept of reinventing the wheel as much as anyone, but sometimes even the positive things from the past can hinder change — especially the dramatic change that many of us have to go through in both our personal and professional lives.

Certainly for me, part of the excitement and appeal of change in life is the attraction of the unknown. However, for many, the concept of the unknown equates to unacceptable risk, it is a scary thought and we end up trapping ourselves in 'cages' of the known — why do many battered and abused women return to their brutes of husbands for instance?

It is the recognition of the existence of that 'cage' that is one of the biggest leaps any of us will make on the road to embracing change and shedding the chains. Just getting over that hurdle of stepping into the unknown the first time confers incredible freedom and makes each subsequent time seem easier, in fact allowing even bigger leaps to be made. It still gives me the jitters though, but it is very much about faith, in yourself and your ability to cope.

I've taken some pretty big steps over the years, the first real scary one in 1985 when I needed to leave the cocoon that was our existence at Mount Cook and do something with my life. I was 25 years old, a double-amputee Duty Ranger giving climbing advice — it was like having to give sex advice but never getting to practise what you preach. I had lived in the tightknit Mount Cook community for a critical time of my life, meeting Anne, having our first child, and developing close friendships that still exist today. But something had to be done — we wanted more from our lives; the call of the unknown, the untapped potential was too great. Anne and I looked at a variety of businesses and careers, but in every case we felt we had neither the money nor the expertise to be able to put our plans into action. However, with what I know now, if we were in the same position again then we would jump into the unknown, rather than just making tentative steps towards it as we did at the time.

Eventually we decided there was nothing for it but for me to go back to school. Packing up the most momentous seven years of our lives and going to live on the smell of an oily rag in a cold hovel at Lincoln was hard but we recognised that it had to be done for us all to grow.

Again, early in 1992, while working as a Scientific Officer at the School of Medicine in Christchurch, those rumblings of unease recurred. It was a great job, very satisfying, but the opportunity presented by a newspaper advert for a trainee winemaker proved too tempting. As Anne said at the time: 'As long as it pays more and you believe you can do it, go for it.' Of course I believed I could do it, I was just thankful it did pay more!

In June 2002 I took a similar-sized step. For 10 years I had worked and lived in the wine industry in Marlborough, had acquired new skills, dealt with new technologies, travelled the world and had a secure income. But life was becoming very full so another choice had to be made: the security and lifestyle of wine, or another step into the unknown — an essential step if I was to take the next leap in my life and make room for brand-new opportunities and adventures. The culture of the industry was also changing so it seemed like a good time to implement the plan that Anne and I had thought through, a plan to leave in 12 to 18 months' time. But like much of my planning I was too impatient to follow it through. Standing in the winery yard surrounded by grapes at the start of the vintage I picked up my phone, dialled my boss and said: 'It's time for me to go.' I gave almost five months' notice: plenty of time to re-engineer the plan, plenty of time to worry about what I was going to do to earn a living to support the family, let alone find the finances to make use of the freedom I was hoping to generate. However, from the moment I did that it felt like I was being let off a leash. Opportunities appeared every day, sometimes every hour.

The hardest part, always, as on the Sky Tower, is that first step. Once that step is taken things that seemed frightening will begin to seem more like the adventure they are. That leap of faith into a new business or career will be seen as the opportunity it really is. But even more importantly, new options will appear, options previously invisible. Of course this isn't about blind faith, that's irresponsible, but faith based on your own clear self-knowledge and analysis — go on, give it a go!

CHOICE, NOT CHANCE

So often when we need or are asked to change we see the negative first. How many times have you heard:

'They need to change first.'

or perhaps:

'They started it.'

It seems that when we are intimately involved in a situation, be it work or home, we are often blind to the big picture. That's where Chapter 9 comes in, 'Learn to stand outside yourself' — often so hard to do, but so essential if you are to see if change is needed.

In my belief, so much of change is learned behaviour — behaviour such as the skill of optimism, which once acquired will increase the levels of achievement and insight possible. Our moods, our attitudes to daily life, are all behaviours that can easily be changed, in the process taking us from a very negative and often health-damaging state back to wellbeing and optimism.

While there are some aspects of our lives that we can't change without being less than true to ourselves, things like our sexuality for instance, there is much we can change. The most important thing to remember is that choice, not chance, is what truly determines where we venture in this life of ours. So go ahead and shed those chains, embrace change and release your potential.

SUMMARY PANEL
Shedding the chains

- *If you don't like where you're at, change it.*
- *Change is an integral part of life — don't resist it, use it to grow.*
- *You are the best person to initiate and create change. Your mind is your tool to do it.*
- *Learn to let go of the past and accept who you are.*
- *Don't live life by chance. Choice is what determines your life path.*

4. Must do, not can do

Every New Zealander I know is immensely proud of the 'can do' attitude of our nation. The concept of number eight wire and 'give anything a go' is integral to being a Kiwi.

THE PIONEERING SPIRIT
Recently, during the course of an interview for a documentary on the Kiwi spirit, I was asked: 'Where does the Kiwi "can do" attitude come from?'

My reply was: 'It comes from our past — from our parents, grandparents and great-grandparents. It was they who arrived in these isolated South Pacific islands; it was they who lived each day with a "can do", "have to do" attitude just to survive, let alone thrive. Those pioneers are so close to where we are now in time, that we all still remember the hard lessons they had to learn; we still remember the sacrifices they made to come here and prosper here. Kiwis are an independent bunch, and I believe we are still pioneers in every sense of the word, still practising that "can do" way of life.'

I'm sure that reply of mine got edited down to 10 words in the doco!

Nevertheless, the crucial lesson that our pioneer forebears taught us was the next step — the step that is truly critical to achieving those really big dreams: I call it the 'MUST DO' step.

'TRUE' SPORTS

Now, if you are a mountaineer you can probably skip this chapter; equally so if you are a bullfighter, into motor racing, or even perhaps a sky diver or base jumper. Why? Well, if you do those sports and are still alive and reading this, then you obviously understand the concept of 'must do'. Because it's in these styles of 'sports' — what Ernest Hemingway called 'true sports' — if you don't have the 'must do' attitude then you run the risk of not surviving the game.

But it isn't just sports that are 'must do's'. What are true 'must do's' are our dreams and their implementation — be they related to sports, family or business. However, while on one level it would be great if everything in life was a 'must do', I think we would probably self-destruct if it was actually so. Therefore our 'must do's' need to be cherished, as they generally take so much effort that they can drain you pretty damn quick: so save them for the things that you are really passionate about.

I guess as Kiwis we tend to be more passionate about sporting feats than many other nations. I've seen spectators apply 'must do' in this arena as effectively as any professional athlete aiming for the top. Imagine you are only earning a modest $24,000 a year, are working eight hours a day, five days a week, and desperately want to go and support your team at the World Cup. To be able to earn extra income and save enough money to travel overseas will definitely be a 'must do' for you. A second job, fitted in around your main job and other life commitments, will help lift income. But to free up thousands of dollars you will need to make sacrifices, giving up both time and spending to generate the dosh. But it can be done, it just comes down to whether it is a 'must do' or not.

THE 'MUST DO' CULTURE

Dotted throughout this book are numerous examples of 'must do', the origin for most coming from my background growing up as a youngster in South Canterbury. It was my upbringing there which developed in me the ethos of never leaving a job half finished (though don't go and look at my house — Anne always says she deserves to be on one of those DIY nightmare shows that are on television these days!).

In particular, the work ethic of New Zealand farmers has always impressed me — they really understand the concept of 'must do'. If there's a paddock that needs working up before the weekend, then that's what will happen, even if it means working late into the night. If there's a lambing round that needs doing, a lamb to be looked after or a calf that requires medication, they will be up all night ensuring it is done. When I was a young farm worker there was many a time I would work well into the night to finish jobs like cultivating a paddock so it would be ready for sowing the next day, or just taking advantage of the good weather. My mum or dad would turn up out at the paddock late at night to see that I was OK, with a bit of tea on board, my very own meals on wheels.

But it was mountaineering, and especially years spent as a search and rescue mountaineer at Mount Cook National Park, that really ingrained 'must do' into my psyche. I guess when you rely on each hand, on each foot, for your life, then you really grow to understand the imperative 'must do'. It may sound a bit cocky or arrogant, but that's just the way it is, the essence of mountaineering.

So that must mean that all mountaineers, skydivers, bullfighters and others with the 'must do' attitude are all tremendously successful in business and life, right? Wish we were, but the hard thing for all of us is taking the next step, applying that 'must do' concept to more ordinary life situations. Practising 'must do' where the result isn't life-threatening but life-enhancing, that's the tricky bit.

In other words, it all comes down to what you see as really important in your life and how you define success — is it where you are now or where you are going?

CATEGORISE YOUR 'MUST DO'S'

I believe that 'must do's' exist in every facet of our lives, they just fall into different categories that's all. I think they operate on a micro, almost invisible, subconscious level (e.g. following the rules of our society, like driving on the correct side of the road, paying taxes, caring for our pets, all those mundane things) to what I call the macro 'must do's', the big conscious decisions that shape how we add value to our lives.

What are your 'must do's'? These are some of mine:

- To look after my family: not so much day to day, as I admit I am not the best at that, but to look after them so as to provide them with the love and opportunities they deserve (which is a heap of both).
- To keep my word. I hate having to take something back — not so much the 'loose lips' syndrome of saying things you regret, but more promising something and then not delivering. For example, I've planned a Cape Reinga to Bluff non-stop bike ride for several years now; I've had to replan it three times, and now I've had to postpone it indefinitely. The event has been advertised in magazines and on TV, but to attempt it now would be to cheat myself and everyone else. So what do I do now? I replan and refocus. In other words, it's still a 'must do', it's just that the time frame has changed.
- To climb Mount Everest. This is definitely a 'must do', and the time frame comes before the ride above because I'm getting older every day, as we all are. However, a 'must do' on Mount Everest needs to be tempered with a 'must survive' attitude. It is so high, so hard, and so marginal for survival that you need to have definite time frames and rules constantly in your mind or it might become your last 'must do'.

- To make a difference. To make a positive difference in the world that we all live in is another really important 'must do' in life for me.

KEEP YOUR 'MUST DO'S' IN BALANCE

The trouble is, there's never enough room in life to do everything; we simply don't have enough energy for everything to be 'must do'.

What we need to do is prioritise our lives so that we can apply 'must do' to the essentials. For further guidance with prioritising check out Chapter 15, which is all about creating balance in life — the balance of roles and goals — looking at what is achievable and what is just too much.

Don't be afraid of committing to those 'must do's' though, they're the goals that really pay off in life.

> **SUMMARY PANEL**
> **Must do, not can do**
>
> - Kiwis have inherited a pioneering 'can do' attitude.
>
> - The 'must do' attitude is crucial to activities in which a miscalculation could cost your life.
>
> - 'Must do's' are for those really important things in life.
>
> - 'Must do's' divide into macro (major life decisions) and micro (non-negotiable obligations) categories.
>
> - Balance your macro 'must do's' with your roles and goals in life.

5. Dream big

We all dream, both during the day and during the night. I've heard it said that those who dream at night wake in the morning to find that it was only vanity, whereas those who dream in the day are the ones who turn dreams into reality. That may be true for some perhaps, but if, like me, you consider all dreams as a type of route map for life, it doesn't matter when they come, for any genuine dream is one we can act on with open eyes and that is when we are at our most dangerous.

EVERYBODY DREAMS

Everyone has a dream of some kind, just ask someone close to you and you will be surprised at the answer. I sat at dinner once with a diverse group of people: an older distinguished gentleman, two young ladies, and shall we say a 'mature' mum of three. While chatting about the infinite variety that makes up our world, the older gentleman asked: 'If you could do any one thing in this world — nothing magical — but if you had any resource, what is the thing you would most want to do?'

I expected a unanimous 'save the world' message from this successful group but the reality was quite different. One wanted to sky dive, another wanted to learn to be a rally driver, and you can guess who wanted health and wealth for her children. My first reaction was to sift through my 'dream library', the list of all those things in life that I really want to do but haven't yet got around to (including some that I may never get around to). Shuffling through those aspirations I recognised that while I have an extensive list, the one thing which is at the root of all my dreams is simple: I just want to be able to make a difference.

It sounds simple really doesn't it, but it is very much the driving force for much of what I do, have done, and want to do in the future.

DREAM LARGE

With dreams, like a lot of things in life, size really does matter. To make a difference you really need to dream big — you need your Paralympics, your Mount Cook, your Mount Everest. You need to dream big, to stretch your horizons, to challenge yourself because that's where growth comes from. Small dreams are useful for getting over a few hurdles, but to really learn, bigger is better. Therefore I think it is essential to always have a big dream sitting there in the dream library (that space you set aside in your mind for the big dreams you are too busy or scared to commit to yet) of goals not yet realised.

Some of us have let those big dreams slip away, but the beauty of dreams and aspirations is that you can always go back to them, reorder them and start again. It doesn't matter how many of these big dreams you have fulfilled in the past, or how many you have let slip away, the essential thing is never to stop dreaming big, never to stop reaching even higher, because the minute you stop, life becomes mundane.

However, don't ever feel that you have to have an exclusive dream, and equally, don't be selfish with your dreams, share them with others. For many, that first step of choosing a dream or a goal is the most difficult. Without experience and the self-belief that comes with it then sometimes it's a bit hard to know what is a big dream, a great goal, and what is mere day-dreaming or underselling yourself.

TAKE INSPIRATION FROM OTHERS

I am frequently asked by people: 'Who inspires you? Where does the urge to dream big come from?' I am always humbled and inspired by the dreams and aspirations of so many others, where they have come from and where they are planning to go. My inspiration comes not only from the achievements of our icons of business, sport and life, like Sir Edmund Hillary and the late Sir Peter Blake, but from the lives of the really small, tough-as-nails people who approach every day, every night, just as you and I do — better sometimes — but are significantly disabled. It is the matrix which they all weave, they all represent, that both inspires and encourages me to go forward in my own life.

Studies by a Bolivian psychiatrist have shown that climbers as a group tend to achieve high scores in novelty-seeking and self-directed behaviours but a low harm-avoidance score. In layman's language, these are all traits that are expressed by setting high standards, choosing difficult goals, and exploring new frontiers. So take inspiration from others, whether you are looking to do something great or trying to dig yourself out of a hole. Read of the adventures of people like Peter Blake and Ed Hillary, of any person who has tackled their own big ocean or mountain. Use the successes and even disasters of others to generate your own goals, at the same time massaging the dream to fit your own personality and moral outlook.

DON'T ASK 'WHY?', ASK 'WHY NOT?'

Approach every idea, both your own and those of others, with an attitude of 'why not?' Don't sit back and judge what others do with the attitude of 'why?' All that attitude does is lead to the tall poppy syndrome, which is essentially feeling jealous of the innovation, passion and success of others. The 'why not?' attitude on the other hand, is confirmation that you are an optimist, proof that you'll go further with every dream.

Remember, one person's definition of a big dream can be just the first step for someone else, and still feel just as big; you can only rate the size of your dreams within the context of your own life and accomplishments so far. Although, as we all find out, the more goals you have knocked off, the more you have achieved, the easier it gets to see the next goal and go out and nail it.

I dream big, cursed and blessed with self-belief and experience. I need to dream big because that is where the challenge in life originates from, that is where the 'must do' attitude finds its outlet.

DON'T WASTE YOUR DREAMS, OWN THEM

The thing I have learned over the years is that for every dream achieved, even if it has an outcome or route to it that you hadn't predicted, you will see the next dream even clearer. I liken it to standing on a mountaintop — each time you do the view is great, and each time you can see further and further into your potential.

My goal of climbing Mount Everest is another dream that will come to fruition, but only if I put the work in, do the planning, and chase the dream with those essential tools: passion and commitment. Everest is big for anyone and even more so for a double amputee. What I need to get me there is a great team for support, inspiration, and to share the dream. I will need real focus so I don't let my eye off the ball as I've been known to do in the past. I need to 'own' the dream.

I'll finish this chapter with a warning: dream big for *yourself*, don't set goals to seek the approval of others (if you do, the dream and your integrity will be in danger — that dream will become the master). So dream and aspire for yourself and the good of others; the payback will be worth every drop of sweat.

SUMMARY PANEL
Dream big

- *Always have a dream.*
- *Size does matter: make sure the dream is big to you, really big.*
- *Take inspiration from those around you, weave it into the fabric of your life.*
- *Live the life you dream of: don't ask 'Why?' always ask 'Why not?'*
- *Own your dreams: use them to make a positive difference in our world.*

6. Passion and commitment: the rungs in the ladder to success

Having the dream is one thing, acting on it is another. For me it is a bit like seeing the tops of the peaks of the Southern Alps glistening in the distance — I instantly know that's where I want to be, but wishing and dreaming by themselves won't get me there. To achieve a dream you need to look at it closely, to plan and find each rung in the ladder to eventual success. In this way, each step up will bring you one rung closer to the top.

TRANSFORM THE DREAM INTO REALITY
Those big dreams that we have nurtured are like castles that we have built in the air, in our minds, but what we need to do now is anchor them, give them foundations of rock and assemble the tools to build them.

However, if like me, you have 'dreamed big' then you know that turning these dreams into reality with plain good old planning by itself isn't enough. If it's something really worthwhile, something that will push you to your absolute limits, then there are two other vital ingredients of success:

1. Passion — any dream without passion is like a vehicle without fuel; without passion, trying to achieve the dream will become a chore, and just like the car without fuel, it will grind to a halt.
2. Commitment — nothing worthwhile has ever been achieved without work, without both commitment and perseverance, a powerful duo.

PASSION, THE FUEL OF DREAMS

I do tend to get a bit passionate about my projects — I always have, and I hope I always will. That early dream, the lure of mountains and climbing, was so strong when I was young, just 12 or so, that I spent countless hours transforming our old henhouse at home in Geraldine into the ultimate 'virtual' mountain hut. Boy did that take some cleaning — yep, years and years of chooks had deposited heaps of manure — but I was determined. Eventually, after months of scraping, cleaning and building, I had my hut: not on a real mountaintop, but even better, at the end of the section. The converted chook house — now premium hut — had two bunks, a real primus to cook with, and all the basic tramping and climbing gear that I owned hanging in it: everything in its place ready for a quick getaway to the mountains. Frosty winter mornings in Geraldine would see me down near my hut, using my second-hand ice axe to chip away at any ice I could find. Hey, if I couldn't get to the mountains, I could at least imagine the mountain environment close to me.

Part of the passion I have for life is tied up with being a committed gear freak. What's a 'gear freak'? Well a sort of 'petrol head' with no car. I love knowing the details of my equipment, how every bit works, and even more importantly, why it was designed that way. I think that thirst for knowledge is a core ingredient in defining what constitutes your passion for a subject or object; it certainly defines a gear freak. The thirst for knowledge is like our physiological thirst for water. While we can satisfy it with a sip, we will always want more; but unlike water, the more we experience it, the more intense is our desire to acquire knowledge, continually feeding our passion.

THE PASSION AND COMMITMENT EQUATION

Passion has been an integral part of the industry that has consumed the last 10 years of my life: the culture of the wine industry survives and thrives on intense passion and commitment.

One of the best things about living at Mount Cook in the 1970s and '80s was being able to wander into the local 'eatery', The Hermitage, and know you were in one of the very best restaurants in New Zealand. The chefs came from all over Europe and New Zealand, as did the wine list. For a country kid it was a revelation to taste great Sancerres, Burgundies, Champagnes and Bordeaux as well as the developing wines from New Zealand and Australia. Thus commenced a passionate interest in that biological medium called wine. Match that with food, an equal obsession (sorry I meant passion), and the regular visits to the Panorama and Alpine Rooms were eagerly anticipated.

By the early 1990s I was continually looking around for an interesting twist to my career in science as the passion for my current occupation was beginning to wane. With the desire to acquire new knowledge in that field steadily diminishing, I needed something that would allow me back into the fresh air but still stimulate the brain. Of all things, reading a Dick Francis novel reawoke in me the passion for wine, the science and mystique of it, so that when a job was advertised for a trainee winemaker for Montana in Blenheim, I was already primed for change.

I'm a strong believer that if you are mentally and emotionally ready for change, for new opportunity, then new directions and challenges almost seek you out.

That advert asked for a person who had a good science degree, life experience, and a love of wine — a job tailormade for me, I was sure. An interview was granted, though I'm sure that it was Andy's (the senior winemaker) passion for climbing that helped get it for me — passion works.

I am thankful that I got that chance to change direction, and especially the opportunity to enter the wine industry at such a pivotal time. It was a time when just having skill as a winemaker wasn't enough: you definitely needed intense passion and commitment to make a real difference.

Winemaking, done right, is such an intense vocation that without great passion and commitment you may as well just be making any old beverage. Initially I was there as a trainee winemaker. Montana was developing its prospective winemakers (and still does to a large extent) from people who had good science degrees and the desire to immerse themselves in the culture. Being a large commercial concern though, each winemaker needs to rely on an integrated team to make the final product — especially if aiming to take on the world, as we were.

It was and is in this aspect of winemaking that the 'life experience' part of the equation becomes essential. It is no use whatever having a great passion to create wines and even the skill to do it if no one will do as you want; because no matter how hard you try, you can't be there 24 hours a day doing everything yourself. Great wines show the intensity of effort and care of every person involved in the process.

The difficulty in making wine isn't in what you add, which you can see and explain to everyone, but in the potential of the grape that you need to let be expressed in the final wine. Every step in the crafting of wine has the potential to lower the quality of the final product if done poorly, and that is frequently a difficult concept to explain. Often it is what you *don't* do that is as important as what you do — and that's where the passion for making the best possible wine is essential. There are a lot of stunningly good wines in this world — I've been fortunate to sample many of them — and the passionate winemaker in me celebrates the intensity of fruit and care in every single one.

The other key criterion in winemaking, as in so many other businesses and sports, will always be commitment: the concept of never packing up or giving in until the job is done. Once again for me, that attitude developed out of my rural lifestyle and family work ethic while I was growing up, and the concept of 'must do' ingrained in me from years of mountaineering. When the grapes are ready to be picked, then picked they must be. But even more importantly, from the moment they are picked, nothing can interrupt the processing flow. The concept of going home while there are grapes in the yard to be pressed, or any other of the multitude of tasks to be completed, doesn't figure.

To achieve the optimum result, passion and commitment are essential, coupled with that 'must do' attitude.

NEVER QUIT ON YOUR DREAM

I recently heard of a saying, 'Winners never quit — quitters never win.' Stickability is what wins wars, wins awards, wins friends and wins respect — certainly mine. Whenever I get in a tough situation and the insidious thought of quitting is creeping into my brain, I commit myself to holding on that little bit longer. Why hold on? Well, if you get into that tight situation where everything seems to be going against you — on the track, in business or in life — when it seems that you can't hang on a minute longer, never give up, because that is exactly the point at which the tide will turn.

For instance, in every bike race that I've been in where I have let myself be dropped just before the top of a hill, I have regretted it. Every time I would think, 'This is just too hard, it hurts too much.' I now know that if I had held on just that second or two more I would have been able to stick with the leading group, but I didn't have enough commitment to the race, to the pain, to the challenge. In a sport like cycling, what's the worst that could happen? You might go so hard you chuck up but that's about it. In fact, it is in those very sports that have an easy 'out' that real commitment is displayed; those situations in business or sport when you can always just say 'stop' and walk away. Which is a hell of a lot different from being in the middle of the Southern Ocean or on the side of a mountain — you always get a helping hand in commitment there as there's no way you can go home. So every time that I have given in to that blessed feeling of relief which occurs when I have backed off,

I have always desperately regretted doing it by the end of the race.

Sure, sometimes you have to quit, but as long as it is losing the battle, not the war, then that's not quitting. Commitment has always been for the long haul, for the ultimate completion of the dream. If a few rungs on the ladder break and need mending or redesigning in the process then get on with it.

> ## SUMMARY PANEL
> ### Passion and commitment
>
> - *Climb the rungs in the ladder to success step by step.*
> - *Assemble the tools to build your dream.*
> - *Passion is like an unquenchable thirst for knowledge, essential to fuel the dream.*
> - *Passion and commitment are two halves of the same equation.*
> - *Never quit on your dream: if you can't walk, crawl.*

7. No fences

How many times in the last year, in the last month, in the last week, in the last day or even in the last hour have you thought: 'I'd love to do that but I can't.' That one little word 'can't' can totally alter the way in which we live our lives, the way in which we enjoy life and the chance of ever expressing our potential.

'CAN'T' AND 'WON'T'

The power of that negative thought comes directly from ignoring and underestimating the value of yourself. Life is a constant juggling act between being told that you can't do things, thinking that you can't do things, and understanding the difference between 'can't' and 'won't'.

Sitting here in Hanmer Springs on our deck, my eye is drawn to the mountain peaks that surround us. I want to stand on each, as every one looks to have a unique way up it, each one looks like it will give a different view, a new perspective on my environment. But I know that each will exact a toll. The reason I haven't yet been up each isn't a 'can't' thing but a 'won't' thing. I will do them eventually, but it'll be after I train (which takes me three times longer than most of you), and it'll be when I can schedule them into the limited time we are all allotted for our lives: that's 'won't', not 'can't'.

'WHY?' AND 'WHY NOT?'

As a kid I got as passionate about my dreams as I do now, the big difference being I didn't then have the skill, or more importantly, the self-confidence to know that I should be out there implementing them. Small-town New Zealand has been responsible for producing some of our greatest dreamers and innovators, but I think it has also been guilty of placing a lid on many dreams. Why? Well, for me it came as much from the naivety of living in a small rural town, expressed as a lack of self-confidence as a youth. It was not so much a matter of dreaming big as figuring out how to put the rungs in the ladder. In other words, a lack of understanding of the power of perseverance.

An example, I guess, is my early passion for motorbikes. For much of my youth I was obsessed by motorbikes, motocross, enduro and trials riding. Frosty South Canterbury mornings would see me out spud-picking — back-breaking work — to earn enough for my first bike (a Honda CG110 I think — totally unsuited to my dreams of becoming an off-road ace as it was a learner's road bike, but a start).

I spent those years dreaming of being World Motocross Champion, but I spent far too much of my hard-earned money on motorbike magazines: I definitely spent too much time reading about my dream and not long enough implementing it. It comes back to the small-town thing again I now realise; not enough self-confidence to pursue my dream as I was scared that when I did people would laugh.

I've certainly put up my own fences and other people have added to them, making those fences of the mind even higher through a lack of understanding that they existed and a confusion between 'Why?' and 'Why not?' The core to releasing your potential — or even getting a glimpse of it — is to retrain the mind to perceive the difference between these stances.

TAKE RISKS

There are some very real fences out there to be overcome as well, the main one for so many dreams being money. Growing up in the '60s and '70s my family was by no means affluent, so the concept of spending thousands of dollars on motorbikes, let alone travel, was never going to happen — not just by spud-picking anyway. I guess I will always regret not trying hard enough, erecting too many fences and excuses of my own which impeded my dream.

Similarly, it is far too easy to hold our children and even our friends back from expressing their potential by being overprotective, by taking 'won't' options that they might or might not pursue and turning them into 'can't' ingrained behaviour.

I once read in a newspaper of a survey that was supposedly done of people older than 100 years; the question put to them was: after seeing so much of life, what was their biggest regret? (Definitely not a question I would like asked when I reach 100.) Apparently the most common answer was that they hadn't taken enough risks in their life; they expressed regret over not taking or making opportunities, regret at being halted by 'fences'.

I see so many missed opportunities from my own past that still create a 'what if?' thought. Although I strongly believe that it is no use looking back unless it is to learn a lesson, what you need to do is turn around and use the lessons for moving forward.

BE PROACTIVE NOT REACTIVE

What I have learned over the last 43 years — and especially over the last 20 as a double amputee — is that for much of my life I have been too *re-active* to the fences put up, whereas I should have been more *pro-active*, for even faster growth.

What do I mean? I don't know about you, but my reaction to being told that I can't do something is like that of the proverbial bull when shown a red rag. It's like kids who are told that the stove element is hot and not to touch it — as soon as Mum's back is turned what do they do? Touch it of course! That's reactive.

To be proactive, you need:

- the desire to go out and find the challenge;
- the desire to change your circumstances; and
- the willingness to take the necessary subsequent actions.

To be proactive, you need self-belief; you need to be unafraid of failure or else you won't be brave enough to try. The 18th-century writer Samuel Johnson said: 'Self-confidence is the first requisite to great undertakings.' The self-confidence to take the first step is the critical thing. Some have it from the start, some need to learn it through experience, but if you don't take on those challenges in life then you'll never acquire it.

Like for many amputees, my life is a continual balancing act between being reactive and proactive. For new amputees, initially life revolves around being reactive to the new restrictions laid upon them, but for many that reactivity soon becomes overshadowed by the desire to test the limits, to be proactive.

The concept of reactive vs proactive is just as valid in business affairs as it is in recovery from a disability.

Any business or life coach will tell you that the most important step you will make is the first one. The thing that holds most businesses and individuals back is the lack of commitment to taking that first proactive step. Without it there is only growth within a sphere of reactivity. To grow outside of that sphere, which others determine for you, you will need to be proactive, you will need to find that challenge, that new idea, and then commit to it.

Phil Doole's ascent of Mount Aspiring and his climbing and trekking feats around the globe have been very proactive achievements. Less than a year after our double amputations Phil was trekking and climbing in Peru.

Here are some examples from my own life where I've managed to be proactive:

- Climbing Aoraki/Mount Cook.
- The creation of new leg technologies with Wayne Alexander, legs like the Alpeds used on Aoraki, and the cycling 'Dashfoot' used at the Sydney Paralympics.
- Retesting and being passed to finish my pilot's licence.
- Having the self-confidence to change careers, stepping away from a 'safe' career to find the new opportunities that abound out there.
- Not accepting the traditional reactive 'disabled' thinking (that of limitations and 'can't'), but instead always thinking 'why not?', the essence of a proactive life.

While so much of our potential is tied to self-belief and optimism, it's probably truer to say that most of our mediocrity is tied to a lack of self-belief and optimism. Remember, you will always spend more time regretting what wasn't tried than what was tried and didn't work.

SUMMARY PANEL
No fences

- *Work out the difference between 'can't' and 'won't'.*
- *Think 'why not?' not 'why?'*
- *Be a risk taker.*
- *Take a proactive not reactive approach to the 'fences' in your life.*

Section Two

Stepping over some of life's stumbling blocks

8. Procrastination: we'll talk about it later

I fill my life up. I like it full to brimming, but full with interesting things. Unfortunately it often fills up with the uninteresting and frequently mundane clutter of existence. You know the stuff — reconciling bank statements, doing your receipts, going for a ride in the cold, drenching rain — the things that we really want to put off, the things that we really don't want to do. When we put them off by inventing more important things to do, or by just plain ignoring them, then that's procrastination, and it is all about the theft of time.

Here's an analogy. The true challenge in making and judging a wine is that continuously nagging thought: 'Is this wine the best possible expression of the grapes that went into it?' Procrastination works very like that: until we get to the end of our lives (or perhaps even just afterwards?) we will not know how important those hours we waste now will be.

REST TIME AND WASTED TIME

Of course, efficiency zealots will always tell you that if you waste time through procrastination then you obviously don't understand the true value of your life and the time-space allotted to you. This is all well and good if you can differentiate between what is genuine procrastination and what is a needed rest because of fatigue, mental or physical. That differentiation can be made in two ways:

1. By experience, especially in being honest with yourself; familiarity with the concept of standing outside of yourself and looking back in helps tremendously in making the distinction.
2. By asking for help and advice to do the first.
   In either case, it's important to check out your total stress load, because if the cause of the procrastination is fatigue then that's an indicator that your life is overfull and you need to start pruning things out; prioritising life to make it more manageable.

Benjamin Franklin summed up the situation by commenting that people who are good at making excuses are seldom good at anything else. This is a bit of a harsh judgement perhaps but it does sum up procrastination rather well. My own preferred saying is: 'Wasted days can never be recalled, though quite often enjoyed.' I must admit that I'm pretty cruised about a lot of things in life; I'm certainly more an ideas guy than a nuts and bolts person, hence procrastinating about the mundane aspects doesn't stress me too much. I believe that if you are going to waste a day, enjoy it. By doing that at least it isn't wasted any more — perhaps not used in a way others would prefer you to use it, but definitely not wasted. I call it recharging the batteries, refreshing the mind. Just think of the last day you did nothing. If you are like me that meant you read a book ('educated yourself'), went for a walk ('trained'), spent time chatting with the family ('communication and love'). As you can see, it's pretty hard to achieve nothing isn't it! These are very different situations from just sitting around waiting for tomorrow to come along, putting off tasks today because you can just as easily do them tomorrow. Unless you have invented a time machine you cannot live your life in the future, though too many do.

CLARITY OF VISION

From observations gleaned over the years I reckon the most significant contributors to procrastination are a lack of direction (a lack of clarity in thinking, i.e. plain old lack of planning) and guilt or fear of a situation. If you are unsure of what you need to be doing, then things generally go downhill from there. It's extremely easy to waste time with woolly thinking or just plain feeling lost. How often have you been in a situation where you were unsure what was expected of you? What did you do in that situation? Many will just muck around. It takes self-confidence to seize the initiative, to think through what is expected and implement it. That could be you.

FEAR FACTOR

By the same token, how often have you been in a situation where you just want to put off an action for as long as possible because it's something that you hate doing (much easier to get it over and done with), something that you feel guilty about or perhaps are just simply scared of doing? I can recall any number of situations when I've been climbing or skiing when I repeatedly put off making a move or starting a run because I'm chicken. I stand there knowing that self-belief got me to this point and my skill and training will get me through or at least keep me safe if I fall, but there is always an excuse not to start. Guilt is even worse. How many times have you put off telling Mum and Dad or perhaps your partner some bad news? Once again it comes down to under-standing that things only get worse with procrastination. Problems rarely disappear, in fact they are just like a bucket of grapes that gets left lying around unprocessed. Like the grapes, problems will ferment into something far worse than if you had dealt with them promptly and correctly. We will all experience many problematical situations in life, so the best thing we can do is practise getting into control mode.

SUMMARY PANEL
Procrastination

- *Procrastination is theft of time.*
- *Distinguish between rest time and wasted time.*
- *Clarify your thinking, and plan for tomorrow.*
- *Tomorrow never comes if you just wait for it — implement your plan.*
- *Is your procrastination based on fear or guilt?*
- *Train yourself to handle the difficult things.*

9. Learn to stand outside yourself

So often we are immobilised by the most minor of criticisms, and equally often we react with counter-criticism and defensiveness, responses which further diminish our effectiveness in achieving the things we want out of life. For me, it is important to understand what others think of me, how others see me, because while I don't necessarily need to change myself for them, I do need to understand the Mark Inglis that they see so I can interpret their comments and advice.

SEE WHAT OTHERS SEE
Looking back I only really learned this technique while I was winemaking. Working in a large winery meant having to understand many other people and myself, and especially how others perceived me. Without that insight it is difficult to interact really effectively with other team members, which is absolutely essential in order to excel.

When you are a winemaker, you need to develop good strategies for handling criticism, as wine is as much about fashion as science — if not more so — and everyone has an opinion; everyone thinks they are an expert. Hence you get accustomed to living in an environment of continual feedback.

I was lucky to work with a company that specialised in helping facilitate change and excellence in business. One of the first things I was taught to do was to get together five or six people to fill in a profile questionnaire that built up a map of how these people saw me and my interaction with others in the workplace. At the same time I filled one out myself and they were compared at an analysis session.

What I learned was that when people meet me the first and foremost thing they see is a double amputee — for many, the first double amputee they have encountered. It is something so far outside their regular experience they can't visualise what it means, perceiving only the disability, not the person and ability behind it.

How about you, would you be willing to see how others see you so as to better interact with them and create excellence in the workplace?

LOOK BEYOND THE CONTAINER

For the first few years of living as a double amputee I really was what people thought — a seriously compromised body — but the thing that I learned was that it was just the body that was compromised.

As hard as it is to imagine, the body is just a vehicle or a container. We are not just our bodies, they are merely a place for our soul or being to reside.

This is a particularly useful mindset to adopt when you are injured or in pain, especially chronic pain. It's a great way of dissociating yourself from the damaged container, giving you a chance to look at the repair and healing process in a more clinical manner.

The best thing to happen to me during my recovery post-operatively was living in the spinal unit at Burwood Hospital. Those people understood better than anyone the concept of living in a damaged shell, that bright minds still find ways to achieve and thrive.

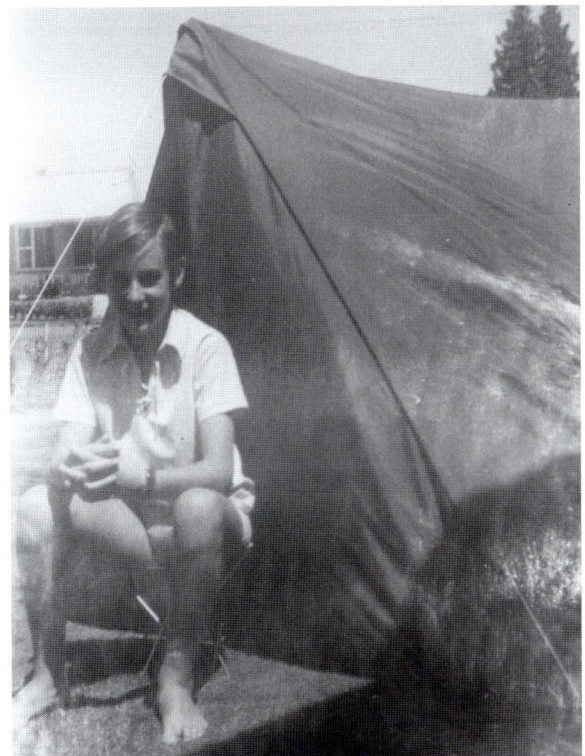

Above The Inglis family team in 2002: Lucy, Anne, Amanda, Mark and Jeremy.

Left You've got to start young: Mark at 'base camp' on the front lawn, Geraldine c.1973.

The dreams and passion start early: at a motorbike show, c.1972.

Above High on Mount Hicks, 1981: the way down frequently looks more difficult than the way up!

The two blurred images (left and below) are the only record Phil and Mark have of the climb in 1982. They come from a film that has only recently been found and developed. Photos The Doole family

Above Mark leading in soft conditions low down on the East Ridge, 16 November 1982. The Nor'west Arch is ominous in the background.

Right Empress Shelf, 8am, 29 November 1982. Phil facing the camera, Mark in the stretcher bag, minutes after being lifted off the Summit Ridge of Mount Cook/ Aoraki.

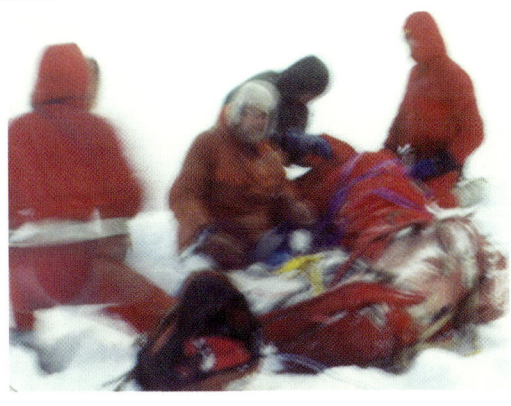

Left Graduation, May 1990 at Lincoln University: the proud recipient of a BSc Biochemistry, 1st class Honours.

Below Haematology Research Unit, 1991: Mark doing an imitation of 'beaker' the lab geek.

Right Testing the 'Alped' climbing legs, November 2001.
Photo Chas Toogood

Below Mark (wearing the Alpeds) and his 'leg man', Wayne Alexander — innovative engineer and friend.
Photo Chas Toogood

Left Aero helmet: getting 'psyched' at the start of the kilo at the European champs, Zurich 2001.
Photo Chas Toogood

Below In the starter's hands, Zurich 2001.
Photo Chas Toogood

Above Mark at 'home', in the snow on Mount Isabel, Hanmer Springs.

Below Race preparation: changing into the cycling legs.

Above Mark and his tools, Hanmer Springs, July 2003.

Below Some boys never grow up, and the passion for motorbikes is still just as strong as ever. The technology that made the Britten V1000, shown here, is now being used to make Mark's legs.

STEP OUTSIDE AND LOOK BACK IN

1990 saw me return to skiing with a vengeance. Although I had tried skiing a few times in New Zealand, trying to adapt walking legs to do the job was a frustrating exercise. Part of the problem was that I had never been a really good skier previously. I had skied lots of difficult runs and snow conditions, but I wasn't a technically skilled skier, so it was hard to understand what feedback I should be feeling. By this I mean once you get really proficient at a sport or technique then you will always know the feeling, the feedback from muscles and limbs, of the correct technique. If you haven't reached that level before, then as a new amputee you have a picture in your mind of what it should *look* like but in skill sports like skiing it's all about what it *feels* like. Without that background it's a bit like groping in the dark. The minute you get it right it's like throwing a switch and flooding everything with light.

At a medical conference in Utah early in 1990 I got the chance to ski with experts. Due to an overabundance of ego (my own) and misunderstanding of their role I hadn't skied with the New Zealand Disabled Skiing Association at all; instead I had tried to reinvent the wheel by devising ways of setting the boots up correctly and stabilising my stumps in the sockets. At the UCLA conference everyone would disappear off skiing for most of the day, the conference business being conducted in the early morning and evening. Left alone to wander the historic town of Park City, the base of three ski fields (Park City, Park West and Deer Valley) I came across the Vietnam Veterans Disabled Skiing Program HQ. One look in the door to see wheelchairs and legs lying around assured me I was in the right place. I spent a fantastic couple of days with them (all I could afford at the time) and learned exactly what I would need to do well when I got home. In fact, I asked to take a photo of a ski leg only to be told it had been built in New Zealand, in my own limb centre.

Needless to say, by the time the New Zealand winter arrived I had the legs and was away with my usual all-consuming passion. After winning some medals at the NZ champs that year (the reality was there was a field of just two in my races: a hotly contested field of two though, and very proud of those silvers and a gold I am too) I had my eyes firmly set on becoming world class. I spent the summer getting some sponsorship and convincing the family that the new boots, three pairs of skis and six weeks away from work in the coming winter would all lead to fame and fortune as an international disabled skiing champion.

After four or so weeks at Cardrona at the New Zealand training camp, I felt bulletproof on the surface, but something was nagging away at me inside. It all came to a head when I saw a video of my skiing. After being told, and damn well knowing, that I skied awesomely well, I saw a stiff-limbed double amputee with little talent and even less grace. I was shattered, terribly embarrassed that I had performed one of the greatest sins (to me) of being all talk and no performance. Equally, I was furious with everyone around me for not telling me the truth. In fact they had, I was just too pigheaded to realise it.

I went on to race poorly in New Zealand and Australia, withdrawing from the team selection. Not that I would ever have been selected — the selectors could see that for me to take the next step I would have had to find substantial funding, give up my career and put my family at risk. In short, I walked away pretty stressed and pissed off.

It really wasn't until I gained those skills of self-perception at Montana that I could understand what had happened. I thrive on challenge, I wilt and waste away without it. When I was continually being praised I stopped trying. However, the praise was for a double amputee doing OK, not Mark Inglis with a dream to achieve.

After being immersed in Montana for four years, winter 1996 was time to get skiing again. Using what I had learned about how people react to me I knew the odd trick to get the best out of situations. Early in the season I headed up to Rainbow Ski Field near St Arnaud and took some skiing lessons. I took on my first lesson with an open mind, determined to ski well by anyone's standard, and, even more important, hide the fact I was a double amputee (easy with some baggy ski trousers). I learned more in the three runs before the instructor caught me adjusting a strap that held the legs on than in tens of lessons previously. I got unadulterated advice and, even more importantly, I ignored my perceived limitations, doing my best to perform each and every activity. Even better, once the instructor knew I was a double amputee and was willing to push any limits, he stretched me and gave me advice that in one day had me skiing better than I did when I had legs. Later that season at the New Zealand Disabled National Champs I skied to a gold in the Masters Grand Slalom. But more important to me was the fact that Pete, my old instructor, didn't realise it was me skiing towards him, my skiing had transformed to such a degree.

'So how the hell did you get that good?' Pete asked.

'Simple mate — on one hand I *listened* for a change, and on the other I ensured they saw *me*, not a double amp.'

Now when you are feeling particularly noxious, really getting upset over something, take your mind outside your container and look back in and do a reality check. Do you like what you see? Is what you see from out there the same as others see? I am not asking anyone to compromise their beliefs but we all need a regular humility check.

Carl Jung once suggested: 'Your vision will become clear only when you can look into your heart. Who looks outside, dreams. Who looks inside awakes.'

INTEGRITY ACCOUNTING

Over the years I have learned a useful gauge for analysing myself and how I interact with others. It's a concept called the integrity bank: a bank in which you have your own integrity account. When you make commitments and keep them you make a deposit; when you act with responsibility and humility you also make a deposit. When you aim low and achieve, you deposit 'cents'; but when you aim high and succeed, you deposit 'dollars'. By the same process, every time you don't achieve your goals you make a withdrawal; you withdraw some of your credit every time you fail to meet a commitment, 'dollars' disappearing whenever your lack of commitment impinges on others.

The integrity bank also reflects the 'what, why and how' of everything you do. For a deposit, the 'what, why and how' need to be dictated by the principles you live your life by — if you are making compromises then you are withdrawing and weakening the basis of a healthy life. For that healthy life I believe you need your imaginary account to be in credit. Treat that credit as the capital fund to help you grow into the future, to help you to interact successfully with others and realise your potential.

THE WIN-WIN CULTURE

The skill of standing outside yourself and looking back in can also be used to fine-tune how you interact with others in business. Often, especially if the business is your 'baby', your dream being nurtured into reality, you may not understand — or won't understand — the messages people are trying to give you.

I think every leader should regularly poll their group with questions that help define how they are seen to operate and compare that to how they think they are operating. One way is the 'Producer, Manager, Leader' poll. To do it, get your team to write down the letters P, M, L, and size each letter to reflect the situation.

- Producer is the worker: how much time do you work at the 'coal face' of your business? How much time do you spend doing the things that you have hired others to do?
- Manager is just that: how much time do you spend managing the business, managing the others in your team perhaps, managing their time?
- Leader: that's more about growing your business or team, looking ahead for new opportunities, inspiring people versus managing them, creating the team.

Your team may see you as P, M, L, but you may see yourself as P, M, L. If that is the case then it's time to sit down and discuss how to fix the situation. Equally importantly, the team need to indicate how they would like to see you for the good of both the team and the company.

You don't have to use these particular descriptors or even stick to three, you could just as easily use things like Mother, Wife, Worker, Lover, Individual — try anything that reflects your priorities. You will find it a simple but extremely powerful technique to help give you a clearer and more honest idea of how you are both perceived and performing. It is a technique that will also help develop an environment of trust, especially if it is done in the transparent environment of a win-win culture.

Win-win is all about creating a situation where both parties come out happy; it's nearly always possible but often needs some small compromise. Perhaps it's buying a house? You need to find the fairest deal through negotiation, not the deal that shafts one party! Wage negotiations, too, are often more winner-loser culture than win-win.

Win-win seems so logical but can be difficult to achieve without trust, especially if people have come from the very competitive winner-takes-all, tough-for-the-loser culture that some traditionally associate with success.

PERCEIVE YOUR BIASES

One of the toughest aspects of standing outside yourself and the concept of win-win is recognising that we all live life with biases. It's by asking for help and input from people we trust that we can see those biases (by the same token, recognising that they will have biases of their own), perceive those habits that we weren't even aware of and move beyond them.

Practise standing outside and seeing yourself as others do on a regular basis in order to achieve your dreams.

> **SUMMARY PANEL**
> **Learn to stand outside yourself**
>
> - *Learn to see what others see.*
> - *Distinguish between the container and the inner being.*
> - *Step outside and look back in to grow.*
> - *Start your own integrity account — manage it as carefully as your money.*
> - *Practise win-win at all times.*
> - *Recognise your biases and grow beyond them.*

10. Some days that glass is just half empty

How many times have you heard motivators and business analysts judge people by whether they see a situation as a half-full glass or a half-empty glass? These days, if you are a 'half-full glass' type of person, you are considered to be an optimist. But if you see situations as 'half empty, and still going down' then you have just been tagged a pessimist. To be optimistic is an enormously powerful attribute, but it is often misused. In fact, in business they say choose a pessimist for your accountant or financial advisor and then have a wildly optimistic marketing and sales staff.

I generally consider myself to be an almost incurable optimist, but there are some days and some situations where all that I can see is that half-empty glass — and it's emptying rapidly too. The reality is that if you live your life seeing only the optimistic view then it is quite likely you haven't really lived, you haven't seen some of the more difficult side of life. In fact, to me, the thought of living life with eternally rose-tinted glasses is a prospect as boring as eating the same food every day. If you can do it then good on you, but I'm sure it is a damn sight harder and less real than having an occasional off day.

RESPONSIBLE OPTIMISM
What I would like to suggest is a life based around 'responsible optimism', a concept based more on positivity, and one that seems to me more practical, more task-orientated than just thinking nice thoughts. I guess the point is that it isn't always appropriate or realistic to be optimistic and there are plenty of examples of situations in which it would be foolish or even downright stupid to be so. How many times have you heard people console others who have experienced a tragedy by saying, 'Everything will be OK,' or perhaps 'Try to be happy.' There is nothing wrong with the intent of the messages, but the timing usually sucks. I've been guilty of overt optimism in the past myself, and probably will be in the future unfortunately, though less often I'm sure.

RAISE YOUR HEAD ABOVE THE MURK
The trick to surviving the odd half-empty day is to learn to be able to get your head above the murk for a glimpse of where you need to be going, and even more importantly a view of where you have come from.

I can assure you, when you wake up on Christmas Day and it is your first day as a double amputee then the cup can look a lot less than half empty. It's over 20 years since I woke up in Burwood Hospital on Christmas Day after having both lower limbs amputated. Bad enough perhaps, but what made it far worse was that in the preceding month I had thought, as a relatively intelligent guy, that I had come to terms with what was going to happen and that I would wake up seeing a half-full cup, a new beginning, a brand-new opportunity.

In fact, I woke up feeling like crap — no other word really to describe the pain, the discomfort and the total reliance on others (those incredibly dedicated nurses who put up with self-centred prats like me). I looked down the bed that morning and all I could see was the 'leg bridge' holding the sheets off what was left and nothing but bed after it.

I wish that back then I could have had the foresight of a guy like Steve Bayley. Steve was an outdoor fanatic, a skier and diver, very talented, but as he will tell you, he knew that he would never have the resources to ski competitively at an international level. Waking up as a new single below-knee amputee from a motorbike accident, Steve immediately thought, 'Now I have the opportunity to ski at the Paralympics.' That takes serious guts, forethought and a dream. It isn't that the Paralympics is easier by any means, the standards reflect the true elite event that it is, but more that New Zealand is an international force with excellent programmes in place for disabled skiing, making the 'bar' to jump over just that much more achievable.

START AT THE BEGINNING

So it is easy to say, 'Get your head above the murk', but what really works? I regularly get asked, 'How do you do it when so many others lie down?' I'm not sure I have any definitive answer to this question, but more a bag of techniques that we can all use. Also, fewer people 'lie down' than many imagine; it is more just that we see disabled people at one point in their rehabilitation and apply that image of them to their whole life — not very fair is it?

So how do you get up? Well, I think the first thing to realise is that you are the thinker of your thoughts — only you. Now from that position of strength it is time to find the positives that always abound in every situation, just a bit disguised on those half-full days.

On those days I always start at the beginning: I'm here, I'm lucky to be alive, and no matter how frustrated or despondent I get, it's a great place to start. I'm lucky to only be a double amputee: if I had spent too much longer on the mountain and if it had been any colder I would be dictating this book, as the frostbite would have got my fingers, and my nose and ears. Lucky also that the stay in 'Middle Peak Hotel' in 1982 was only 13 days; if it had been too many more then I would not have been here at all. I know my survival is due to pilot Ron Small and mountaineer Ken (Digger) Joyce's skill on day seven in air-dropping, in very marginal weather and flying conditions, bags with the means of survival: food, fluids, sleeping bags and stove.

Furthermore, although the cup can seem to be half empty in retrospect, rarely should any metaphorical cup be anything but half full when you are looking forward to your future. For people to go from being pessimistic to optimistic isn't a matter of winning a lottery, having good luck, or some other external catalyst, but simply flicking a switch inside which lets them see that they predisposed themselves to having a bad day by how they approached it.

OPTIMISM AND PESSIMISM ARE CHOICES

The first step to becoming a responsible optimist is to recognise that much of the time we tend to think pessimistically, sort of like on autopilot. Just as with any problem in life, and more especially those difficult ones we don't want to acknowledge, the first step in nailing it is recognising that there is a problem — ask any drinker, smoker, overeater or gambler.

A technique that is helpful is to challenge yourself, to wave that red rag, not at a bull but at yourself. Once again it boils down to the difference between being reactive to problems versus proactive. Reactive thinking and actions are frequently generated by the pessimistic outlook, whereas proactive thinking is nearly always optimistic in nature. This approach also allows you to put any problems into perspective — how important are they in the scheme of things? What is the pessimism doing to your stress levels? To make a conscious decision to challenge yourself is really refreshing, perhaps a bit intimidating but nevertheless refreshing. Think how often making a decision feels like a load being lifted off your shoulders — optimists live life with that very feeling most days.

The second step is to remember that you are the thinker of your thoughts, that all the half-empty pessimistic days are created by you, in your mind. You are the one who can easily reverse the flow — hell, they're only thoughts! A single thought or reversal of attitude will not change your life in one go, but the effect is cumulative, it puts you in the right frame of mind to see other opportunities and foster more optimistic ones.

CIRCUMSTANCES REVEAL CHARACTER

I have to keep on holding back from saying 'I'm being realistic' or at least using that statement as an excuse to think that circumstances are what it is all about. In fact, circumstances in themselves don't make a person, they merely reveal them, and that is precisely how an optimist should regard each day, each new challenge. When things get tough our true character really shows through.

The image I have of myself and the driving force to improve myself comes from seeing how I have reacted in difficult situations in the past. For many years I shut out the events of the 13 days sitting in that frozen hole at nearly 3600 metres on Mount Cook in 1982 for the very reason that I wasn't happy with how I performed. I semi-jokingly say: 'Give me the situation again and I'll do it even better.' Why? Because we learn. I saw how I reacted in extreme situations — the months in hospital, the amputation, these are things I could deal with even better now because with those experiences behind me, those 'gold standards' of pain, extreme cold, malnutrition, of seeing death so close, have revealed to me my inner self, a self that I think I can improve upon.

Lastly, if you are like me, half-empty days hurt. It's time to go easy on ourselves and others on these days. Too often it is easier to be a cynic; there is so much pain and injustice in the world that we quite often focus on what's wrong, stuff that we cannot easily fix, if we can fix it at all.

You will always find what you are looking for in this world. If it is someone to blame for the wrongs, you will always find a scapegoat. By the same token, if you are out to hunt down some good in the world, then I'll guarantee you will find that also.

On those half-empty days always remember to look at your situation with a bit of humility and a lot of humour — you'll be amazed at how quickly they can turn into half-full ones.

SUMMARY PANEL
Some days that glass is just half empty

- *Practise being a responsible — not impractical — optimist.*

- *You have to get your head above the murk to see the positive side of life.*

- *Use the concept of challenging yourself to overcome situations.*

- *You are the thinker of your thoughts; it's you that can change those thoughts.*

- *Optimism costs nothing, pessimism can be very expensive.*

- *Circumstances reveal a person's character, they don't make a person.*

11. The terrible P word: planning

Do you know your biggest weaknesses — in business, in sport, or in everyday life? I know mine, which I think is essential, as knowing my weaknesses gives me a chance to work on them, to reduce their negative impact on my life, and in fact to create a positive impact instead.

KNOW YOUR WEAKNESSES
Write a list of what you think are your main weaknesses. For me they are:

- planning (too little)
- avoidance (too much)
- impetuousness (I just get bored too easily, I want things NOW!)

Lack of planning, avoidance and my impetuous nature are all intimately linked.

The planner's mantra will always be: 'Plan your work and work your plan' — great advice for life but not so easy to practise. Or, as carpenters say, 'Measure twice, cut once'. Unfortunately I'm the sort of carpenter who takes a guess and chips away until it fits! Mark Twain put it like this: 'Plan the future because that's where you are going to spend the rest of your life.'

PUT YOUR PLAN IN PLACE

I find that while I can see where I want and need to be, I frequently have trouble with planning far enough ahead. I never seem to have a 'life plan' sussed, because as soon as I do I feel constrained and want to do something different (that impetuous part of my nature coming to the fore). So for me a good life plan has to be one that helps me identify and make the most of opportunities that come along, even when they take me on a completely different tack from the one I had anticipated.

For the athlete or business competitor, planning is the groundwork to success. It is the why, the what and the how of our dreams and challenges. One of the best planning analogies I know is the ladder. Every dream or goal can be looked at as an object on top of that wall: to get there we need a ladder, and planning forms the rungs to that ladder. In addition, by constantly evaluating and assessing your plan you can avoid the most embarrassing of mistakes — that of putting your ladder against the wrong wall! There is nothing worse than putting all the effort in only to find you have gotten the wrong result.

EVALUATE, PLAN, ACT

Far too often though we try and skip from the start to the finish. We try to leap up the ladder without touching enough rungs. We try to achieve the goal without the work — but more importantly without the planning — to succeed.

For an athlete the steps are:

- Show your mind and body the sport or activity.
- Show your mind and body the skills needed.

- Develop your strength and endurance so you can last the distance.
- Show your body and mind the speed and intensity that you need to succeed.
- Lastly, train in the environment, apply the lessons to the real thing and you will have a winner.

For a business the steps might look like this:

- Show your mind and body the business or activity (evaluate the proposition thoroughly).
- Show your mind and body the skills and knowledge needed (train, educate yourself).
- Develop your strategies to ensure your business will grow in size and strength to last the distance (business plan).
- Show your body and mind the intensity of effort and commitment that you need to succeed.
- Lastly, test the product/business in the environment, apply the lessons, passion and training to the real thing and you will have a winner.

See some similarities? It doesn't matter what sphere of life we operate in, the basic principles of creating the plan and then living the plan are the same. I call it the evaluate, plan then act routine.

TIME ZONES

When I made up my mind to commit myself to the Sydney 2000 Paralympic Games the first thing I did was go to Tony Catterick, my cycling coach, and describe the dream. Tony has been an internationally ranked professional cyclist, and these days I am smart enough to seek out others who have 'been there' as there is no sense in reinventing the wheel (I've done that too often).

The first thing Tony asked was why? Why put myself (and an ageing self, sportwise, at that) through the commitment needed to lift my body and performance enough? Why add to the pressure of work and family? Easy — I knew I could do well, I had the self-confidence, the essential self-belief that meant I knew I could be one of the best in the world, and it was an opportunity that was unlikely to come my way again. What I needed Tony for was to help structure my intense and diverse life, to tell me when the balance was wrong, to ask me the hard questions, such as: 'What the hell did you do that for?' or 'What do you want to get out of that event or that day?' They're the questions every business competitor and every sports athlete need to be asking themselves every day, but frequently avoid.

Now avoidance is different from procrastination. As I've said, procrastination is more about wasting time — time you can never recover. Avoidance, however, is best described as the 'ostrich phenomenon' — that is, burying your head in the proverbial sand and hoping like hell difficult situations will just go away (in fact, procrastination is a technique that people into avoidance end up using by default). Unfortunately problems never do just go away — the best way to deal with the tough situations in life is to plan around and through them.

A planning tool I now use to help me through my tendency to avoid things I don't like — frequently things that I need to deal with whether I like it or not — is using time zones. Time zones, moveable on a quid pro quo basis, are just a tool for building the discipline needed to complete tasks in the best possible manner. We all have diaries, written or electronic, especially if we lead a busy life. All time zones do is pre-book time to complete important tasks, which is a great way of ensuring you accomplish the hard things as well as ensuring you don't miss out on the important things.

Once again everything comes back to clearly seeing what roles you need to fill in life. What are you: an employee? a parent? an athlete? a partner? What? Make a list of the roles you need to fill in life, giving real thought to prioritising them as well, both in the short and long term. I can assure you that for me my perceived role in life changed dramatically in the lead-up to the Paralympics. So much commitment was needed that the family slipped from the top, and work slipped to the bottom. But this was only short term, a matter of manipulating time zones, swapping them around to attain short-term goals that increase the payback in the long term.

While I may seem addicted to challenge, the selection of each challenge is all about the balance of my roles and what benefit it will bring my family and myself in the longer term. On paper you can do it: list those roles you need and want to fill, now and in the future, and then list your dreams and goals. It's by comparing these two lists that you will achieve a far clearer vision of the planning path you need to take. I find it's also a very useful tool for managing my tendency for being a bit impetuous — it is like a base to come back to, a regularly reviewed rock or foundation for my life.

Therefore, these days, if something looks like a great idea, as much as I would love to jump in boots and all, I do the evaluate, plan and act routine. But even before that, I go back to review the time zones available, the roles I'm required to fill, and ask the questions:

- Is this more important than what I have already planned, what I have already highlighted as 'must do's'?
- If so, what do I have to give up or shift around to do it?

I'm sure you will find this process beneficial.

RESOURCE PLANNING

So you have planned for yourself, but what about for external resources? No one lives in a vacuum, so any effective planning exercise should look at the way our plan integrates with others, how best to use external resources such as the expertise of others or perhaps the availability of the materials to grow.

Much of my inspiration and the tools to achieve my goals can be attributed to 'external' resources. Wayne Alexander at Britten Motorcycles has been both the expertise and the supplier of resources for many of my projects. I often use him as my 'head and leg man' — head man because of his expertise and innovation in thinking out and engineering new ways of tackling the challenges of amputee climbing, skiing and cycling; leg man because he creates the physical resource, the specialist legs that provide me with both the ability and the inspiration to achieve more.

It is important to admit that you can't do everything yourself. Sure, the whole concept of doing something entirely by yourself is great, the feeling of achievement can be enormous. But with the help of others, with the sharing of the dream, even greater results can be achieved.

Too often great ideas dwindle into moderate-sized ideas due to a lack of resources. Don't allow a lack of proper resource planning to shrink your dream.

> **SUMMARY PANEL**
> **The terrible P word**
>
> - *Know your weaknesses so you can plan around them.*
> - *Plan your life, live your plan.*
> - *Make sure the ladder, your plan, is against the right wall.*
> - *Evaluate, plan, then act.*
> - *Use tradeable time zones and roles to help prioritise and organise a framework or base for your life.*
> - *Plan to ensure sufficient resources, of both people and materials.*

12. Communication: easy to say, harder to do

I communicate superbly well. Yep, I can talk to myself all day, let myself know where I'm going, what my current challenge is, how I'm feeling about it, what dreams I have in the pipeline and how I'm feeling right now. It's a real pity I'm not so good at sharing it with others!

COMMUNICATION OR MAKING NOISE?
Honestly, I have always thought I am great at communicating, or at least I always want to talk about stuff, and in fact I'm a bit of a motor mouth at times. Unfortunately, effective communication is a bit more complex than that. In fact, the world's motor mouths are some of its poorest communicators.

William Shakespeare expressed the distinction this way: 'Give every man thy ear, but few thy voice.' Now call me a bit dumb if you like, but I would have thought a great poet, playwright and orator like Bill would have wanted to offer his voice to plenty of people. Sounds like a winemaker asking people to please only look at the wine, not drink it. But the man has a point, the mouth can override the ear and put obstacles in the way of communication.

PUT YOUR BRAIN INTO GEAR
The Spanish have a saying: 'Speaking without thinking is like shooting without taking aim.'

As far as speaking without thinking goes, I may be the holder of the endurance version of the 'Foot in the Mouth' trophy. Anne keeps on having to give me a clip around the ear to get me to re-engage the brain. Here's one situation as an example. I was speaking to a group about mentoring, a favourite hobby-horse of mine (I wouldn't have done half the things I've done or gained a quarter of the insights into my potential without mentors) and someone asked whether I would be racing at the Athens Paralympics in 2004. Good question.

My usual — planned — response goes something along the lines of this:

'I hate the concept of old, slow athletes; it always seems obvious to everyone but the athlete themselves that they should have given up last year. Sure, you don't want to miss out on that performance of a lifetime, but old and slow is a bad look.

'Paralympic sport is becoming increasingly competitive, especially the training-intensive sports such as cycling. To be at the top, time in Europe every year and minimal interference from trying to make a living is essential. That in itself makes it extremely difficult for me.

'In Paralympic sport the athletes do tend to be a bit older: by the time you have had your accident, been through the journey of recovery and rehabilitation, the years are advancing. It isn't unusual to see athletes in their thirties and occasionally forties, depending on the sport.'

Well that kind of answer can be a bit long-winded so I thought for this particular lady I'd just shorten it to: 'You never know when some young professional cyclist will have a car accident, lose the odd limb and then blow us old buggers out of the water.'

As it turned out, her son (Anne is whispering this in my ear as I'm in full flight) — a top young cyclist — has just been killed in a car accident. It was one of those occasions where what seems like a joke to you can actually (inadvertently) hurt someone. Of course, I wasn't to know about her son, but to me that one encounter will always remain ingrained in my mind as an example of the value of sticking to your communication plan.

PRINCIPLES OF COMMUNICATION

If you are lucky enough, you can spend years at university obtaining the highest degrees in the science of communication, and there are plenty of 'gurus' out there making a significant amount of money telling our corporate community and others how to communicate. All of which is probably not a lot of use to you or me, so here is the Mark Inglis short course in the fundamental principles of communication.

A working definition of communication might go something like this: 'Communication refers to the act, by one or more people, of sending and receiving messages that occur within a context, has some effect, provides opportunity for feedback and is often distorted by noise.'

What's said can't be unsaid

Like my off-the-cuff remark about road accidents, one of the key rules of communication (opening your mouth) is that whatever you say has been said, you cannot take it back — it's called irreversibility. The unfortunate thing is that lots of us spend far too much time trying to retract or make excuses for things that just shouldn't have been said in the first place.

Communication goes beyond words

Another critical rule is that if you have at least two people in the same place, irrespective of whether they say anything or think they are communicating, they are.

The lesson here is that you don't need to say a thing to convey a meaning or a message.

Inform and compliment, don't patronise

While we spend a lot of time using communication to compliment and inform, it's essential to do it in a manner that's non-patronising. As a double amputee, I can assure you that I have encountered every sort of patronising approach you can imagine — more often from adults than kids. If only people wouldn't associate a lack of limbs or mobility with a lack of intellect, although fortunately this kind of behaviour is less common today than 20 years ago. The most powerful and positive use of communication is to inform and positively reinforce actions, given of course that truth is paramount.

Criticise constructively

Another purpose we use communication for is to criticise, but for it to be effective — at home or at work — then you need to criticise constructively and positively.

For example, which sounds better: 'I don't like that black outfit' or 'You look great in those light colours, they suit you much better than black.' I know the 'correct' answer is the second one, and I hope for your sake you do too! Remember, if you need to criticise or deal with conflict, then put as many 'I' messages in as you can. Personalise it to yourself to take the sting out of difficult situations.

Now suppose you are making a presentation to a group with a colleague but the approach or style they are using is all wrong, and you just know it will 'bomb'. To criticise your colleague directly may well cause offence, so try an approach like this:

'I did a presentation a bit like that a few weeks ago and it was pretty good, but what I found was that this [other] approach worked much better. Want to try it?' Or, 'Could you try it for me this time?'

When you are contemplating criticising just give some thought to this — how many statues to critics have you seen? Not many I bet. Criticism certainly helps us grow but if it is poorly delivered the messenger may be shot!

Obviously sometimes the personalisation approach isn't that workable, such as when debriefing a team after a loss. The essential component though is for that 'failure' to become a lesson; to focus on the fix, once the broken bits have been identified.

DON'T JUST HEAR — LISTEN

As William Shakespeare suggested, listening is one of the crucial skills, powerful for both you and those around you. Just think, if you don't listen then the information you will impart to the world will be derived from only one source — you.

What are the benefits of listening? Consider some of these:

- You learn, gain knowledge, and grow yourself.
- You avoid problems by picking up hints before things come to a head.
- It helps you relate much better to others — no one likes people who won't listen.
- You'll be able to help others much more effectively the more you understand them and their situation.
- Lastly, the more you listen, the more you will be able to influence people and situations to mutual advantage.

SEEK TO UNDERSTAND

When trying to communicate, remember to recognise and understand the culture of the audience. I don't just mean race, but age, religion, wealth, everything that builds the culture of each audience. As I write I am presenting elements of the *INZONE* Roadshow around the schools of New Zealand. We (Rob Hamill, Steve Dean, Peter Doake, Chris Ward and I) tell the inspirational stories of Kiwis like John Britten, Suzie Moncrief (of 'The World of Wearable Art'), Sir William Hamilton and his revolutionary invention, the Hamilton Jet, Rob and myself. Every audience we present to displays a different culture depending on where we are in New Zealand, what type of school it is, the ages of the children and the other myriad components that make each community unique. The audiences are very honest — much tougher than adults in many cases — so you really need to have your act together to be able to communicate the messages over 90 minutes (90 minutes of hard school seats as well).

As you might expect, part of my talk describes my dislike of and total incompetence at team sports as a kid — a story that I normally put a lot of humility into when describing. However, on one particular day I didn't, I let my early dislike for some of our team sports show through, in effect denigrating some of the fine sportspeople in the audience. Now with adults, I would get and give back some 'robust' ribbing, but because I had misjudged the culture of the audience they almost froze. I then had to work very hard to bring back a level of humour and respect to the talk. By misjudging the culture of that audience I had overlooked one of those critical elements of communication: once it's been said, it's been said — you can't take the words back.

COMMUNICATE YOUR BUSINESS PLAN

Businesses, with possibly the exception of the odd 'one-man band', cannot succeed without planning and communication of that plan. Look within any organisation, no matter what size, and communication will be one of the key elements of the organisation's success or failure. Why? Because for any organisation to succeed several conditions have to be met, conditions that everyone in the team needs to understand clearly, such as:

- A specific and clear desired result: that's what we are all here for.
- Clear guidelines for behaviour and the operation of the organisation.
- Resources are identified and standards are specified.
- Accountability and roles of team members are defined.
- The consequences of actions are understood.

However, while it is important that everybody within the organisation is pulling in the same direction, it doesn't mean that they have to agree on everything. One of the classic mistakes in organisational communication is the assumption that everyone has to be mates to make the business work. Which is not true at all — in fact, that would generate a very stifling organisational atmosphere. What is needed though is respect for others' points of view, a concept which is often only paid lip service to in competitive environments. It is the importance of listening coming to the fore again: the ability to understand another's position is critical if everyone is to be understood and everyone is to win — surely the object of the mission.

Good luck with getting your message through — it does take work though and not just chatter.

SUMMARY PANEL
Communication

- *Just because you are making a noise it doesn't mean you are communicating.*
- *Speaking without thinking is hazardous.*
- *Whatever you say has been said, it can't be taken back.*
- *You don't need to speak to communicate.*
- *Inform and compliment with integrity and respect; criticise the same way — the objective is to learn.*
- *Practise and train yourself in listening.*
- *Understand others first, then make yourself understood..*
- *Just like people, businesses need to communicate effectively.*

13. Frustration: learning to live with things you can't change

So many people ask me what it is like being a double amputee: 'Is it painful?' 'Do you take your legs off at night?' Or commonly: 'What's the worst thing about being an amputee?'

Well, for me, the worst thing about having no legs can be summed up as frustration — the frustration of losing an element of freedom and the frustration of losing the immediacy of life an impetuous person like myself values so much.

WORK AROUND WHAT YOU CAN'T CHANGE
What do I mean? Well, when I look at a hill or peak now, instead of being able to tear straight up it as I was prone to do, I need to go through my mental checklist:

- Are my stumps up to it?

- What am I doing tomorrow or next week, and how will it be affected by any damage I do to my stumps today?
- Can I actually do it? (With my level of self-belief, the answer is generally yes.)
- Do I need to train?
- Is it worth it?

Questions like these need to be ticked off before I can commit to some of what seem to be the simplest things in life (this was especially true back when I was a new amputee). They need to be ticked off and understood to enable me to achieve the outcome I want (and, in fact, expect) and also to find the balance in life that I desire.

In other words, I have to change what I can change, be proactive where I can to sidestep and overcome problems, and learn to work around the things I can't change.

The reality is I will never grow new legs, and in my lifetime technology is unlikely to find a way of giving me legs the equivalent of those I lost. Understanding that is the key to moving forward, to being part of the innovation that will create improvements in technology for future generations.

Frustration still stays with me though, partly because I have the 'gold standard' of full mobility (myself before the amputation) to compare my current mobility with, even with the improvements I have made and am still making.

NON-ACHIEVEMENT AND FRUSTRATION

As mentioned earlier, I have always dreamed of doing a significant ride, Cape Reinga to Bluff, 'non-stop'. That dream has had to go on hold for three reasons:

1. I have taken on too much this year, with *INZONE* taking a lot more time and energy, resulting in my taking my 'eye off the ball', that is, losing my focus, stepping outside of my plan.

2. I just haven't been able to do the miles, the hours on the bike, that are needed for an elite ride. I know I could go out tomorrow and survive the ride, but it would be slow and not what I wanted, which was to showcase elite Paralympic sport.
3. The real dream, the number one goal, is to climb Everest. To do that in the next 18 months will take all my energy and planning — everything that dilutes that, dilutes my chance of success.

This is the third time I've had to postpone the ride for the reason that I'm not fit enough (because of a chronic hamstring injury and hence lack of miles), and I haven't planned my life well enough — I've been too greedy, trying to fit too much in.

Equally as bad, in fact like compounded frustration, is the cancellation of my September 2003 trip to Shishapangma in Tibet. The reasons were the same as those for the cancellation of the ride. The core of the frustration, the non-achievement for both situations, is an unrealistic expectation of my own abilities and those of others.

The most frustrating thing about this type of situation is dealing with what you see as failure to live up to what you have told others would happen. So how do you deal with the frustration of non-achievement, how do you take that feeling of helplessness and turn it around?

REDUCE FRUSTRATION BY PLANNING BETTER
Eighteen years ago I was also dealing with frustration. After getting legs and returning home to Mount Cook village I started work as the Duty Ranger for Mount Cook National Park, a role that I had helped out in before the events of November 1982. Essentially it was managing the visitors to the park on a day-to-day basis — giving advice on activities that ranged from climbing the highest peaks to a 10-minute walk; managing the intentions book and climbers log, ensuring everyone was where they should be in the park and not in any danger; and monitoring the weather station and information.

My frustration revolved around watching everyone else doing what I used to do, as well as I used to do it, and not being able to do it any more myself, or at least not being able to do it as well. That was a situation where change was needed, and a change in environment was what resulted. Perhaps I could have continued on there, but the frustration of not rehabilitating as quickly as my impetuous and impatient character demanded meant more stress and anxiety than I was prepared to live with.

What I have learned is that much of the frustration in life evolves from illusion, a lack of reality. At times of frustration it is important to take a step outside ourselves, look back in, and do a reality check. Usually we'll find that the frustration arises from a lack of the planning process, that 'evaluate, plan, then act' routine which helps turn frustrating situations into situations that will deliver a positive result. Because frustration and the sense of discouragement which goes with it so often comes from a blurring or changing of your vision, you need to continually refocus on the plan, keep on re-evaluating the dream to ensure it is still what you want. Just remember, it comes back to a balance between just dreaming about those big dreams and the proactive planning that is essential to achieve them.

INCONSISTENT EXPECTATIONS

By now I hope you can see that frustration is ultimately derived from expectation. If the expectation is too high or differs from the outcome, frustration is frequently the result.

In a group situation frustration from inconsistent expectations is generally a function of communication. Each member's strengths, weaknesses and expectations need to be clearly understood. Everyone in an organisation needs to be fully informed of the results that are required or expected, and how they will be achieved. Each person needs to understand and be committed to the 'dream' — that's the level of communication necessary to eliminate frustration.

Frustration generated by inconsistent expectations can be extremely damaging to a team — and it's so easily remedied by communication and negotiation.

SUMMARY PANEL
Frustration

- *Work around the things you can't change.*
- *Frustration generally comes from non-achievement; asking why you haven't achieved is the most important question.*
- *Plan better — remember to stand outside and look back in; reality reduces frustration.*
- *Inconsistent expectation is at the core of frustration.*

14. What to do if it all turns to custard

Life isn't all roses that's for sure — you certainly don't have to tell me about it. When you set your sights high, the fall can be tough. Sometimes things just don't work out no matter how hard you worked at them or how much you wished they would fall into place. Nonetheless, I believe there is only one possible failure in life and that is not to be true to the best you know you can be. Or as Confucius, the fifth century BC philosopher put it 'Our greatest glory is not in never falling, but in rising every time we fall.' Both ideas bring together the concept that failure to achieve a goal should ultimately be looked at as yet another lesson in our lifelong learning. But as suggested by the word 'lesson', you need to be prepared to learn from the mistakes.

GET BACK UP
I seem to specialise in turning parts of my life into custard. In fact, one of the lessons I try and share with others these days is why my life has

so often been like that. On the other hand, hopefully one of the things I have also been able to show is that I specialise in getting back up each and every time as well.

As my Mum always told me, it's all about 'biting off more than you can chew' — that's the time when things start to go to custard. Well I've just about choked on some of the things I've done because when you go out and attempt the impossible on a regular basis, as most athletes and many businesspeople do, there will come a point when it just gets too much. You become increasingly tired, and eventually if you keep on 'getting up' you will break down. Some see it as overtraining, others as overcommitment — business or sport, the result is the same: custard.

LEARN FROM YOUR FAILURES

While many people see me as successful, I see myself as 'a work in progress'. Perhaps I tend to be a bit hard on myself, but I reckon I haven't even started yet. In fact, I see success as not where I am, but how I've got here, which is all about getting back up again and stickability. The scary thing about that though, is that I realise I have some significant failures to come — things that are probably going to hurt mentally, financially, and almost definitely physically.

While the last thing in the world you want to do is expect or seek failure it is pretty important to learn some of the reasons behind it, how to see it coming, and what to take away with you from each failure or lesson.

Unfortunately, I've had some very public failures, which means you can't hide them away and pretend they didn't happen. As a winemaker, for instance, much of your vintage, especially in a 'challenging' year (you aren't allowed to use words like bad, crap, wet, cold or frosty, the marketing department don't like it), is all about crisis management in a stressful environment. In wine, when things turn to custard, then generally two things happen:

1. You get bad wine — a bad advert for your company and your expertise — revenues fall and hence profits (unpleasant all round really).

2. Wine or juice goes down the drain — the worst possible scenario as that is potential income never to be accessed, let alone profit.

When stuff like that happens, in most businesses the initial response is 'Heads must roll now!' — the classic knee-jerk response (ask any sports coach who has been dumped after the team lost).

But that isn't the right response for growth, especially if you want to continually improve your product. Sure there must be discipline procedures in place, be it a sports or a corporate team, but if the big stick is used too regularly then the result is the concealment of future mistakes, which is far more harmful than being clear and open. In the wine scenario, if there is a culture of fear and recrimination, a hidden mistake could mean thousands of litres are affected instead of mere hundreds — all turned to custard in fact.

The learning approach isn't easy though, as a balance between discipline and learning needs to be struck. Factor in the passion so many people have for their craft or sport — passion to the extent that they look almost physically hurt when mistakes are made — and you have a very fine balance indeed.

However, the learning attitude is critical to surviving failure just as the ability to get up again is the key to eventual success. In December 2001 I attempted Mount Cook/Aoraki again, after an absence of 20 years. That December climb, as it turned out, was a significant learning experience, as this excerpt from *No Mean Feat* will demonstrate:

> Alarm goes at 11pm though no need really. I can see the lights of the film crew, hear Charlie up and about, worrying about the wind and keen to get away. Repack everything done four hours earlier, think harder about it and repack again. Breakfast, always hard at midnight, but manage to stuff down some bread and Weet-Bix. More cameras, more people, and feeling a bit stressed and nervous. Stumps have that tender feeling that gives me a bad feeling. Even being up so early we still get away late (12.30 am) as

Charlie is reminding me, so I remind him I was happy to go three hours ago. I really don't think the guys have understood my requirements, my limitations, but what the hell, we're here now.

At Plateau you need to rope up from right outside the hut as the first slope leads right into a crevasse field. From the first few steps I knew things weren't going to be easy. The freeze we were relying on had only partially occurred. The snow wasn't hard enough for me to stay on the surface. Even the footprints formed the day before hadn't frozen enough for my climbing legs; they were continually punching through even deeper. In the dark (actually the light of our headlamps) this causes two problems: extra energy and effort are involved in plugging 'new' steps; and, worse, being continually slightly off-balance causes tearing and rubbing of the sockets.

So in that strange half light we descended a few hundred metres in the tracks and then put the snowshoes on. The plateau is a huge ice field lying under the eastern flanks of Mount Cook, Tasman, Dixon and the other main divide peaks. It is about 1.5 km from Plateau Hut across to the mouth of the canyon the Linda Glacier has formed.

I had forgotten how far we had to descend straight after leaving the hut; two big partially frozen snow slopes. The snow that morning was perfect for those who had legs but with every step, with or without the snowshoes, I struck a difficulty of some sort. I really wished I had someone in front to make small, really firm steps so that the two-piece Terminator legs could sit nicely in them rather than being the very unstable platforms they were proving to be in those conditions. Someone to take the pack weight would have been great too.

Once we were almost across the Plateau and into the mouth of the Linda Glacier we struck the first frustration — wrong route. We followed the wrong set of steps and ended up in a crevasse field unable to go forward, 'bluffed' as trampers would say. I must admit thinking and yelling out loud to Woody and Wayne up in front, 'What sort of bloody guides are you?' That wee excursion was only 10 or 15 minutes out of the way at the most, but in my nervous state it seemed like half the mountain. I knew I had only a fixed amount of time on my legs, so every small incident that 'wasted' that time was as painful to me as pulling teeth.

As the morning wore on we wound our way up through the maze of crevasses . . . The most difficult bits were those that I had predicted — teetering along arêtes (knife-sharp narrow ridges) with huge slots either side. It was damn lucky it was dark and we couldn't see into their depths. The few steep steps were a bit of a challenge with only one axe and a Leki pole, but I didn't have an easy system to swap the poles for ice tools. It's one of those things that seems simple on a warm day at sea level, but in the dark, when you are ice cold and wearing all the paraphernalia associated with glacier travel, it's an energy-sapping pain. We only stopped momentarily through the lower Linda as it is just so dangerous. I guess if you don't know the climb you can just cruise, but all of us except Wayne were cursed with knowing every ice cliff hanging over us and every accident that has claimed a life in this area.

Eventually we stopped, once we were past Teichelmann's Corner and the main avalanche danger area, to eat, or at least try to (my PowerBars were frozen solid and so was I soon after). Charlie put some clothes on. I didn't drink as it was too much hassle and effort to get my bag off and dick around — which actually showed that the effects of not having eaten enough food were kicking in. Quite amazing really, as on the bike I would never let my body get into that state. I religiously drink and eat at the right times and, as a consequence, I am able to ride for hours on end. This time I didn't really have my act together so I didn't get the fuel.

I was sure that the Bowie Ridge bivvy site was near and we would have a good rest, plenty of food and perhaps a hot drink. So a long trudge up for another hour, but it seemed like several as I was still punching in through a crust every few steps, getting more and more tired, and really wrecking the stumps. Bowie Corner when it finally arrived was really cold and windy. Then the bloody helicopter came in to film and blew me about, which didn't help. I found it really difficult to get clothes on and off, let alone lever and wire the crampons onto the legs. It seemed like I had to

What to do if it all turns to custard

take more clothes off to get more on and by then I was really cold — not enough fuel in the tank for sure.

I hadn't been that cold in years, my brain just wasn't in the right space. The cold and tiredness started to bring on hand and stump cramps. A few shots of Cramp Stop helped, but I knew then that it was probably over. I didn't tell anyone of course. I thought there was still a chance that once I had rested and warmed up the growing pain and cramps would go away. After all, you can see the summit from there. I knew that the next few hours would be extremely difficult as the prospect of failure had already crept into my mind.

From the Bowie the slopes steepen into a chute that avalanches from the Gunbarrel, the icefall just below the summit ice cap sweep. The Gunbarrel dominates the upper Linda area and the Linda Shelf and you must keep moving, like in the lower Linda, to lessen the chance of being caught by a deadly ice avalanche. From there you traverse the steep and exposed Linda Shelf to the gullies leading up to the summit rocks.

Once up and moving on the crampons a few things were very obvious — I was moving slowly, and wherever the snow had that damn breakable crust it hammered me. The stumps felt like they were walking on glass, and below the Gunbarrel is no place to go slow, let alone stop. Every five metres or so we would hit a bit of crust and every time I broke through, frequently dropping to my knees. Then I would need to pull myself up using the Leki poles, wrenching the stumps and cramping my forearms and stumps. Once upright I then needed to pull the leg with the crampon up and out of the hole. Putting the foot down again was agony. After a few steps the pain would settle in to become the background norm and I would just carry on.

One step then another, but none of the rhythm of old, none of the athletic elegance of bouncing around on those great legs, just a continual stumbling through a mist of pain with flashes of white-hot intensity.

All I could think was that after years of dreaming, planning and filming, the whole thing was going to crap because of me and my stumps. Not Wayne's leg design, the weather, or the conditions (sure they all contributed), but me. Having Whetu and Narly around just compounded everything, more people in the Gunbarrel going slow because of me — so I 'pulled the pin'.

I yelled (actually more sobbed) to Charlie, 'Time to stop Charlie, we need to go back and get the camera chopper into Bowie Ridge.'

I dropped to my knees and chanted over and over again, 'It's not supposed to end like this.' I was inconsolable. It shouldn't have ended like that; it needed to end on top of Aoraki/Mount Cook, not at the start of the Linda Shelf where the real climbing begins. I always used to hate the walk in, or the drudge work before the real climb, and this time I not only hated it, it also wrecked me. Bugger.

I'm grateful that I have been able to keep on learning lessons as I go on in life. That day in December 2001 reminded me that I am disabled, and it has helped me understand how I live my life as a dichotomy between being able and disabled. I sometimes tend to forget both aspects, especially the disabled bit.

So what did I do? I sat down and listed what went wrong and why; what I needed to change within myself (both mentally and physically) and how I needed others to change as well. I also listed the things I couldn't change and tried to think through strategies to go around them.

The lists went a bit like this:

What went wrong:

The core problem was the abrasions and blistering of my stumps caused by:

- Climbing in conditions unsuitable for the Alped limbs.
- Carrying too much weight.
- Travelling too far between rest stops.
- Not eating and drinking enough.
- Not asking for help.

- Feeling too much pressure to perform. I let the dream become the master rather than taking ownership of the dream.

What I needed to change was:
- To carry less.
- To get even fitter; to be the fittest person on the mountain.
- To climb like the hare in the hare and tortoise — go fast but have lots of stops (I know the hare didn't win the race, but the climb wasn't a race).
- Get my hydration and food right.
- To pick better snow and weather conditions.
- To find techniques to let me do more work and power through my stumps, to heal faster.
- To understand *why* I was doing this (the challenge, the pioneering of new limbs and a bloody good idea) and for *who* (me).

What others needed to change:
- I needed to communicate better my strengths and weaknesses so the team members could more clearly see what would help and what would hinder.

What I couldn't change and what to do about it:
- The fact that I was a double amputee — no amount of wishing would get me a set of legs that would work like those of 20 years ago. I needed to be smarter and more humble about my abilities while remaining totally confident in myself, asking for help earlier if that fitted with the what, why and how of my dream.
- The weather and snow conditions — I just had to

> keep on checking and accept only conditions that would let me achieve my dream.

So I went home to Renwick, spent time working on the sockets, finding creams and strategies to help heal the raw stumps, and got back on the bike to keep the fitness up.

Several times each day I would check the weather maps on the Internet, looking for that pattern of high pressure with cool southern air that would give clear skies and the essential freeze. Many people were surprised that I went back a mere three weeks later, on January the 6th and 7th, 2002.

What I had been able to do in that three-week period was clearly see the stress that I had put myself under and how that stress had compromised my performance, both in decision making (letting others make the decisions for me — inappropriate decisions) and in physical terms. It was all about learning the lessons and getting back up.

TOTAL STRESS LOAD

In my view it is stress and how we manage it that is the primary cause of so many of our problems. Stress both before, during and after a situation, be it in sport, business, or just life in general.

It has been shown that some stress is essential to achieve your potential — ask any winemaker, if you don't stress the vine you don't get the best grapes (although I'm convinced the management, sales and marketing teams believe that if you don't stress the winemaker you won't get the best wine). However, when the body is placed under stress, it alters its hormonal balance. Compounds such as adrenaline, testosterone, glucocorticoids and mineralocorticoids increase in production while other compounds decrease. It doesn't matter where the stress comes from — money, family, training too hard, biting off more than you can chew — stress is still stress and it accumulates.

With some stress in our lives we perform with greater energy and increased awareness — part of the 'fight or flight' reaction to stress. Too much stress though, and those beneficial anti-stress compounds will start to decrease in output, and that's when we start to get into trouble. This level of stress has an effect on our whole metabolism including the rate at which our cells grow and are repaired and the production of cells in our critical immune system. Hence we get injured and sick, both physically and mentally.

The crucial concept to be aware of, for those of us who push the limits, is 'Total Stress Load' (TSL). TSL is a combination of lifestyle stress, emotional stress, training stress, and event or competition stress. Being aware of TSL helps us to define the sources of the stressors, enables us to find and hopefully maintain an equilibrium, and avoid succumbing to the effects of overstress — that is, when it all turns to custard.

Top-class athletes quickly learn that to be able to handle the stress load of training and competition, their emotional and lifestyle stresses need to be minimal.

Let's look at some of those stress components that make up our TSL:

Lifestyle stress

While many people might assume that this just means having a stable economic base, that's not the real issue — the real issue is time. I've been lucky in that I have had a successful career as a winemaker. While it paid well, almost every event I took part in during those years was in spite of the job. When you work eight to 14 hours a day in an environment in which passion and commitment is essential then it adds significantly to your TSL.

Even now, with a career that means I have more time at home to train, I travel so much that fitting bikes onto planes and training hours into busy schedules in unfamiliar cities is almost worse. What I have swapped is secure income for some more time but less secure income, and a stress load I am more able to manage (hopefully!)

Emotional stress

This is possibly the most difficult of all the stress components to control but that's human nature I guess. If you are suffering times of emotional stress then use exercise or training programmes as a type of therapy. It isn't always easy though — if you are like me, when you are riding, running or walking, the brain is going nineteen to the dozen analysing your life. It takes conscious effort to soothe the mind. Essentially you need either to learn to meditate or else immerse yourself in the minute technical aspects of the exercise. Whenever I am out riding I spend every second analysing my pedal stroke, my heart rate, and revelling in the scenery.

Training stress

Training the body is stress. Physiological training only occurs from the relationship between stress and recovery — your performance comes from that recovery. No one got to be great through either recovery by itself (you just get fat that way) or by overtraining (training too much too fast without recovery). Balance, that's what it is all about.

Competition stress

Unlike many people, I cannot compete very often. This is partly because the opportunities to compete against other disabled athletes are rare in New Zealand, but equally because I become so passionate about the competition, about my performance, and living up to my own standards, that to compete often absolutely trashes me mentally. Most likely this is due to the stress of unrealistic expectations, but as I have said before, if you are going to do something, do it big.

Stress is a vital component in competition though. If it wasn't stressful then it would be a pretty poor competition. If there wasn't an element of the unknown then competition would be as boring for the participants as it would be for the spectators.

It's the management and harnessing of that stress that's essential. It's using it to slot you into the 'zone' that is the critical power to harness from stress. I can tell you days out, sometimes weeks out from an event, how positive competition stress will be for me. There are times when I have failed well *before* an event but, dumb as I am, have continued on to fail *in* the event by not living up to my expectations. This is almost always because I've gone into the event knowing damn well that I haven't been true to myself, haven't trained enough or correctly, have cheated myself. So when I turn up to the event I'm as stressed as hell, which has a further negative impact on performance, resulting in things seriously going to custard.

So even if you aren't an athlete, use the concept of Total Stress Load to manage your day-to-day life. But importantly, if you still can't seem to get a handle on it, still don't have that control, go get help. I should have done just that many times in my life. I wish that after losing my legs in 1982 I hadn't been so pigheaded in not asking for it.

JUST RELAX

There are a number of ways in which you can help yourself though. One useful way to manage the anxiety and stress that is generated and adds to our daily Total Stress Load is 'progressive relaxation'. I first used the technique when doing yoga to stretch my skinny limbs as a young runner and climber. Back on Cook in December 2001, that's how an old friend helped me to refocus my thoughts after that painful 'failure'. It's easy, just lie down somewhere quiet, close your eyes and sequentially tense every muscle in your body BUT just after tensing it, let it relax completely — eventually you will be just a large mound of jelly, totally relaxed. For a start try it on your lower limbs. Tense every toe and relax; all the muscles in your feet, then relax; then the ankles, calves and shins, working your way up. Obviously you would think a double amputee like me would have a significant time advantage over others with so many fewer muscles — well not quite. Granted I don't have the muscles, but I still have the cauterised nerves and sensations of toes and ankles. So to fully relax I have to spend time relaxing muscles that I don't even have — not fair really.

The other way to refocus that I find works is meditation. I'm too much of a cynic to buy into much of the more esoteric spiritual side of techniques such as Transcendental Meditation. But I do believe in the power of meditation, the concept of the simple repetitive chant (done quietly so I don't scare the pets) and subsequent emptying of conscious thought, allowing the mind and then the body to completely relax.

These days I still haven't learned all the lessons, I still overload myself, but I guess that is just my own fault. However, I do have a range of techniques and tools to help. So much of stress and crisis management is common sense, both before and after the situation. Which probably indicates that 'common sense' isn't all that common.

TAKE CONTROL OF STRESS

People seem to be proud of being under stress. I've been guilty of it myself, especially as a winemaker. You'll hear winemakers around the world tell their tales of 18-hour days, weeks on end, as if it is some kind of initiation rite. At the same time, ask anyone if they would like less stress in their lives and they will always answer yes. I believe that stress is very much created by ourselves, either internally or reactively, and it is up to us to control how it affects us.

Think of money, for many of us a significant stress component in our lives. But some people can live on minimal incomes with no apparent stress. They enjoy life and wouldn't trade it for more work or stress no matter what. But for others who earn perhaps a hundred times more, dollars rule and stress their lives. Surely if a defined level of income was required for a stress-free existence, then everyone below that level would be a gibbering mess. Conversely, everyone above that level would be blissfully stress free. I know why it is a significant stressor for me, as so many of the challenges and dreams I harbour rely on significant funding to be done properly. You can't climb Mount Everest on a shoestring — everything comes in units of $10,000 it seems, and lots of them.

How we understand and cope with the small stressors in life reflects our reaction to the significant stressors. Amanda my daughter loves the rain and, like me, revels in magnificent storms and snow. But many others feel depressed by rain and foul weather, and will even move their families to escape it. As you can see, stress is relative, and so too is the way we manage it.

Using the TSL concept to locate where the stress is coming from and how it accumulates will give you the tools to understand that stress is an indicator, a siren that something isn't right. In other words, stress is not necessarily a situation so much as a way of thinking. The idea is to be proactive not reactive. Change what you need to change, what you can change, and don't spend too much, if any, time beavering away at the past. Live now and for the future — *especially* when things turn to custard.

SUMMARY PANEL
What to do if it all turns to custard

- *When you fall over the most important thing is to focus on getting back up.*
- *Learn from your failures — spend time working out what went wrong, and even more importantly, how to fix it.*
- *Be aware of your Total Stress Load. Manage it day by day, even if it means asking for help.*
- *Find ways (like progressive relaxation) to reduce anxiety and refocus, especially after a perceived failure.*
- *Taking control of and managing stress is a personal responsibility — it is your choice.*

15. Balance: essential on the bike, on the cliff and in life

I was recently reminded of the movie *The Karate Kid* and a scene in it which I think sums up the role of balance in my life. There's a bit down on the beach where Mr Miyagi sends his pupil Daniel into the surf to practice his kata (a flowing series of linked moves). The waves rolling into the beach are continually knocking Daniel down, frustrating him and causing him strife. He turns around to complain to Mr Miyagi and sees the old man balanced upon a pole performing the 'crane' movement.

Which are you? The pupil or the master? How many times in your life have you felt like a Daniel — never keeping up, always struggling against the waves that are knocking you off balance, disturbing your equilibrium and causing you to continually play 'catch up'? Or are you a Mr Miyagi — in balance, full of power and elegance, on top of your game and making every move count?

TRAIN FOR BALANCE

Balance in life has so many physical connotations for me, from the obvious aspect of living life on stilts (prosthetic legs) every day, to balancing on a steep ice or rock wall as a climber, to tackling that tricky mountain bike move, to mastering the graceful carving turns of skiing. But the real skill of balance lies in fitting those physical skills into a life that requires even more intellectual and time balancing.

Sure, anyone can easily achieve balance in life by giving up various of its components, but that I believe is selling yourself too cheap. The essence of balance is to find that fine line between doing as much as possible while still leading an empowering life.

Whenever I look back at the video footage of early 1983 as I was fitted with my first prosthetic legs I am reminded of the physical component of balance. After the amputation on Christmas Eve 1982 I had been fitted with thigh-length plaster casts to control the swelling and set me up for a rapid return to mobility. After a fortnight new casts were put on, these with sockets for the attachment of short pylon prostheses. There was no knee action as the casts were once again thigh height, but the idea was that with the pylons attached I would be able to get up out of the wheelchair and walk between parallel bars in the gymnasium. Not a bad idea but I must say I didn't really take to the whole exercise as it was extremely uncomfortable to put my whole body weight (which was bugger all — I was skin and bone) through the casts. Also, because I had lost so much muscle up there in Middle Peak Hotel, my arms were more like sticks than useful supports. First time up and my head began to spin, my heart hadn't had to push blood up that high for about nine weeks or so. The room began to sway and it was time to drop my backside back into the wheelchair.

Oh yeah, the wheelchair. Well, being the gear freak that I am it was just a new toy. Typically, I was disappointed that I had the 'economy' model, but within hours of having it I was planning some modifications and a few speed accessories. Living in the spinal unit as I did for many weeks until the legs were made, it was impossible not to immerse myself in the culture of the wheelchair and develop proficiency in its manipulation. Skill number one: balance. To get around you have to be able to pop a wheelie anywhere and at any time. In fact, you very quickly learn skills such as balancing on the back wheels (very comfortable) using only one hand, so you can hold a stubbie of beer in the other — an essential life skill.

However, achieving balance in a wheelchair can be both a painful and humbling experience. There is only one place you go when you overbalance, well only one place that matters — yep, backwards. As well as bruising pride, the back of the skull can take quite a beating as well. Actually, the wheelchair gymnasium at Burwood (back in 1982 anyway) had the ingenious and technologically advanced system to prevent damage of two ropes hanging from the roof with a loop on each end that went around the back of the wheelchair, thus saving you from that last 300 mm, the painful bit.

Needless to say, I was probably more enamoured with the wheelchair than with trying to stop the room spinning, so I could stagger painfully with rigid legs down some parallel bars, just to please a sadistic physio.

From getting the 'real' legs in February 1983, balance, predominantly physical, was always an issue. Small things like uneven ground, jostling in a crowd, or even a couple of glasses of beer (frequently used as an analgesic), all became big balance issues. Being a new double amputee dramatically restricts the number of things you can apply your energy and passion to. Your life revolves around the fit of your rapidly changing stumps (hour by hour, let alone week by week) into the sockets. As I said in the opening chapter on challenge, the analogy of 'one pair of shoes' was never so appropriate as then. Falling was always a pain. Not just painful when you hit the ground, but also the twisting uncontrolled movement of new stumps in hard sockets, and the humiliation of being down on your arse and stumbling back up like an ungainly new foal. Physical balance is still a challenge for me now, but one to be attacked and enjoyed, rather than simply suffered through.

So, what's the point of the story? Well, balance is a learned skill, a skill that takes practice to achieve. I believe that balance, both physical and in life, isn't a finite thing, but a dynamic situation which continually changes, just as the equilibrium of a balance beam changes as you load up the scales.

THE BALANCE PYRAMID

I find a strong analogy between balance in life and balance in wine. In fact, I use the same diagrams to illustrate the concept of balance in each:

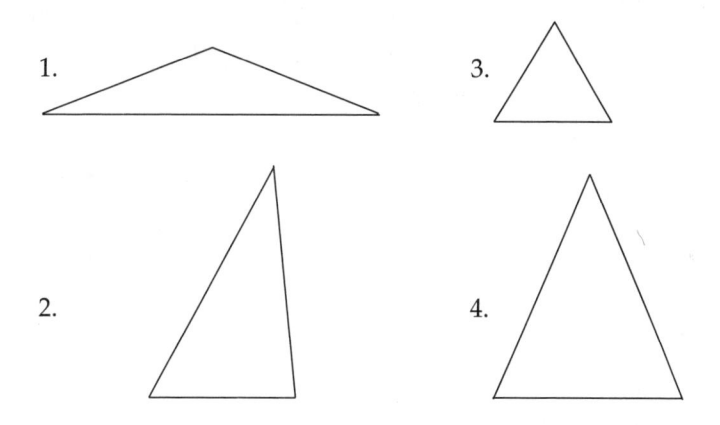

Whether I think of a wine, or of life, I think of a pyramid, in two or three dimensions, and perhaps even the elusive fourth dimension as well. The height of the pyramid equates to the intensity of your life, or the intensity of flavour in the wine. The base line equates to the structural components that make up that life or wine.

Let's take a riesling as an example. The left point of the base line is the acidity of the wine, the right point of the base line is its sweetness, how 'dry' it is. The apex reflects the fruit concentration, the quality of the grape. Ideally the three align as an equilateral triangle, each balancing the other. A late harvest or dessert wine would reflect (4), a wine in balance even though there is a lot of acid and sugar; the fruit intensity is equally high, hence a big triangle, a large internal area. A table riesling is more like (3), still balanced but at a lower intensity, and hence a smaller area. A riesling too sweet and acidic for the amount of fruit concentration, a low-quality wine would look like (1). A sweet cloying wine, with heaps of potential but without the acid to balance the sweetness, is like (2).

Life can be configured that way as well:

1. Depicts to me a life without quality. The base is broad but nothing much is being built on it. In life balance terms it's in a type of balance, but empty and wasted in my view.
2. Stress is taking over here. Too many things are happening in the life without the base strength to call on. This could easily represent an athlete overtraining, a family with too many commitments, and even me some of the time. It's getting ready to 'fall over'.
3. This life is in balance. As much is being fitted in as the base strength can handle; just like
4. Where the greater base strength means far more can be fitted in.

Picture each of these in 3D, imagining that the volume of the pyramid is the sum of your life, and so find your own present balance.

But how do you know how much bigger your pyramid can get or even how big it should be now? Once again we come back to balance, to pushing the limits and swaying back before going too far.

To do this exercise yourself try analysing what I call your 'roles and goals' in the way I explained in Chapter 11. First list the roles that you occupy in life, such as partner, parent, work role or sporting role, and then rewrite the list, ranking each role for importance. What you are doing is creating a life job description, though it is only a snapshot. To do this really effectively you need to do as I outlined earlier and create a short-term and long-term role list.

Now list the goals that you want to fulfil. Go through that dream library that we all have, rank them in importance and then rank them in achievability. Perhaps some need to be completed before others or perhaps you will find some that are redundant.

Once you have a bit of practice at this list-forming and the subsequent balancing of roles and goals, you don't even need to write it down any more. You may find, like me, that you continually review the lists in your mind — something you can do anywhere, at any time.

Now for the hard part. Place the ranked lists side by side and see what fits, what is really important, and what resources you have at hand. Use the lists to create those triangles. Remember, the height is all about how many things are going on in your life, how many roles and goals you have to juggle, and the importance you place on each. The base is the support you have from others, the back-up you have from your own training and skills.

ROLES AND GOALS SHOULD BALANCE RESOURCES
If your life looks like this:

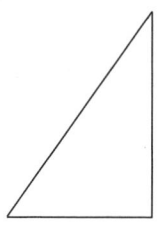

then you are going to need to either prune a few roles or goals or obtain more resources to end up with a life in better equilibrium. The base is too small and lopsided, perhaps meaning not enough support from others (have you asked for help?) or not enough skills and training. The peak is simply too high for that base.

I know from experience that I can survive and thrive even when my pyramid looks like the one on the left below, but not for long. I guess it represents pushing the boundaries, but only as a temporary measure generating the growth to end up in the better position of the right-hand life pyramid.

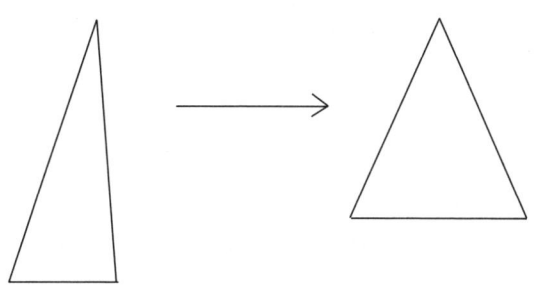

Another analogy that might help in finding ways to achieve balance in your life draws on the seasonal business environment. For much of my life I have lived in cultures that depend upon seasonality: at Mount Cook, the summer climbing and tourist season and the winter ski season on the glacier; and in wine, the ultimate seasonality with vintage forming a critical stressor for everyone involved. The common thread is how businesses like those perceive and manage their year. Do they:

1. Treat it as the traditional cyclic boom and bust, and take the stress and cash of the high season to help offset the dry times of the off season? or
2. Establish a base-line trade that means profitability all year so the boom of the season is the cream on the cake — cream which means that if it all gets too much you can back off and say, 'It's not essential for the business survival,' thereby giving an out, and therefore creating more balance to their existence.

Some prefer the boom and bust. They take off for other climates in the off season, have their rest and find their balance. But I think the most robust businesses and those that offer the best balance to life are those like (2). When you are on top of your game you can always handle the busy times by postponing tasks that you have kept up to date, thereby giving yourself some time and space to lap up the cream. I think a balanced life is more like (2) as well. Surely we are better working away, laying the groundwork, so that when hectic times hit we can either make the most of them or step away from them, keeping our life balance pyramid optimised at all times.

I am regularly asked to speak to people who have been unemployed for a long time. The first thing I ask is whether they actually want a job or are they happy with their lifestyle on the dole. Unfortunately many are more than happy with their unemployed status, because the job that they would like to do (and attached large salary) is unattainable without effort. Once again it is a situation where the expectation of an individual isn't based on any sense of reality. Regrettably, too many don't understand that the price of any success in life is all to do with discipline and hard work. These are the elements that contribute to the intensity and strength of your life's balance triangle.

> **SUMMARY PANEL**
> **Balance**
>
> - *Train for balance in all aspects of your life.*
> - *Aim to keep life as that optimised pyramid, the strong base balancing its intensity.*
> - *Fill in or prune back your life roles and goals until you are in balance with your resources.*

Section Three

Lessons to be learned from sport

16. Race yourself: the secret to winning

Typically New Zealanders are considered by themselves and seen by others as being sports mad. Sports mad we may be, but we certainly aren't totally fanatical, as are so many other cultures around the world. Try being in the States when the Superbowl is on, in India for any cricket test, or in Brazil during World Cup Soccer — even our most ardent rugby fans pale in comparison. However, while sport polarises our communities with parochialism and passion, we are lucky that it has always been the passion for the performance in the sport itself that has been dominant, unlike the passion that is expressed as violence in so many other cultures.

SPORT OR RECREATION?
I frequently feel a bit of a hypocrite as I am regularly asked to speak at sporting dinners and awards — me who has spent much of his life avoiding traditional sport. I always tell the story of studiously avoiding

sport at school, or at least team sport. Apart from being the skinny runt that I was (I avoided nearly all rugby and was pretty hopeless at hockey, and no one in Geraldine played soccer in the late '60s and early '70s), as I've said, team sports always frustrated me. My frustration derived from a combination of feeling guilty about not doing well enough and at the same time being critical of others as well.

However, I realise now that the essence of my dislike boiled down to my personal definition of sport. The dictionaries define sport as an activity for pleasure, competition or exercise. Recreation is generally defined as agreeable or refreshing occupation, for relaxation or amusement. The two are overlapping but there is an element missing from the sport definition and possibly from the recreation definition too, and that is the element of challenge and risk.

To be hard-nosed about our national game, rugby is now a profession for most high-level players, and undoubtedly a profession many kids also aspire to. Sure it is sport by any conventional definition, but not necessarily what I consider a 'true sport'. As I suggested earlier in this book, the concept of 'true sports' is one based on challenge and risk, and predominantly conscious risk — that is, risk that is predominantly under your control. 'True sport' is a concept based on the consequences of poor performance. In true sports those consequences involve the possibility of paying the ultimate price — of paying with your life.

There is no shortage of examples, and I guess degrees of challenge also. From rowing the Atlantic, where in earlier races it was expected that one in nine competitors would lose their lives (odds like that are no longer tenable in 'races'), to climbing Mount Everest, where currently almost 10 percent of climbers attempting the mountain die and four percent of summiteers die on the descent. For Kiwis the Atlantic and Everest are perhaps some of the better known activities, but what about bullfighting? That is not necessarily thought of as sport here but is certainly considered one in Spain and South America. Or what about base jumpers, parachuting off cliffs and buildings, and extreme kayakers? To me, these are all true sports — even though for many participants the dollars involved are pretty important too, as these sports are frequently their careers as well.

Sport and Recreation New Zealand (SPARC), the national sports funding agency formerly known as the Hillary Commission, has recently made funding available for some non-traditional sports, in recognition of Sir Edmund Hillary (after whom it was originally named). The funding is for sports such as mountaineering and adventure racing, in fact any activity that stretches the limits of human endurance and innovation. However, its main focus is still on the traditional Olympic and team sports, effectively eliminating a funding opportunity for more non-competitive sports. In fact, for most New Zealanders, the common conception of sport revolves around activities of an opponent-based competitive nature. In the vast majority of these opponent-based sports, someone needs to win and someone needs to lose. For me that scenario is only a very small distance from the bloodthirsty gladiatorial culture of ancient history.

It is my belief that genuine or 'true' sports and the rewards that stem from them are based on achievement, rather than solely on the outcome of an adversarial combat.

RACE YOURSELF, THE KEY TO WINNING

The essence of achievement-based sport is to race yourself. That's where true growth comes from and is also, I believe, the secret to winning. If you are on the starting line of a race and focusing on your competitors, if you are looking across the line and your primary thinking is based around statements like, 'I'm going to beat you today', then what you have just done in my opinion is put a lid on your performance for the day. What you need to do instead is *think*. Use that great tool, your brain, to visualise the win, to visualise the performance trapped inside of you, instead of visualising just beating the other participants. That to me is real sport — it is where true personal growth and achievement come from.

I've spent time with several great teams, such as the Vodafone Warriors, the Canterbury Crusaders, teams where the sport (and profession) is a combination of skill, perseverance and brutally hard physical effort. These are both teams which operate within the sports that have a strong 'opponent' culture, but which also operate within an achievement culture, a culture of personal and team responsibility. That certainly isn't an easy thing to do when so much of the sport is all about hard physical domination of your opponent. These teams achieve that balance by effective communication, which means that each of the team members understands the desired result and their role in accomplishing it, while at the same time they interact with great synergy in that environment of trust built on responsibility. That is why teams like the Crusaders and the Warriors, and I'm sure other successful teams irrespective of which sport, succeed.

Recently there has been great debate over a woman gaining entry and playing in a men's professional golf tournament. There have been cries of 'unfair', 'stupidity', 'why?', and very few sentiments of 'give it a go — why not?'. Why is this? Mostly it seems that those who don't want her to play against the men claim that it will lower the standard of competition. But if she qualified, how could it? Others claim she will not make the 'cut' (the first elimination round). So what? Enough men don't make the cut — that's why it is an elimination round anyway. Others ask why she should be allowed to play in a men's competition (actually because there are no rules preventing it, just tradition), when men are not allowed to play in women's competitions (they are smart enough to have rules). In my view the very heart of why she should play is because she is aiming high — she is doing it to improve her game. Whereas for a professional male golfer to play in the women's tour would indicate they are aiming low, not high. That they are doing it to beat others, not looking at stretching themselves. This is another example of what I see as the disparity between the philosophies of achievement-based versus competition-based sport. Achievement is all about growth, competition is totally about a short-term result.

ACHIEVEMENT-BASED COMMERCE
The same thinking can and needs to be applied to your business. The principles of achievement-based 'competition' are as valid in the

boardroom, the shop or on the factory floor as on the field, road or mountain. It is no coincidence that many very successful sportspeople continue on to equal success in business. They take the lessons they have learned about planning, passion, commitment and achievement into their lives. It was sport that gave them the opportunity to have those elements of their character revealed.

Businesses, like sports teams, thrive in an environment of clear responsibility and roles, within a culture of effective and free communication combined with a healthy dose of passion and commitment to spur the common goals and dreams along.

INTEGRITY IN SPORT AND LIFE

Every time we turn on the television or look in the sports pages of the paper we see instances of cheating in sport. Most commonly it's drugs to enhance performance but cheating has also been seen in match-fixing for gambling and other monetary motives. Paralympic sport isn't immune either; drugs are extensively tested for, with the occasional positive showing up. As far as the Paralympics are concerned, classification into the most advantageous class brings with it opportunities for athletes to make their disability seem as bad as possible to give them the greatest advantage — is that cheating? I think so. Especially once it crosses the line of truth. A classic example came to light in Sydney at the 2000 Paralympics. Several members of the Spanish mentally handicapped basketball team were later found to have no intellectual disability. In fact, they were professional basketballers back in Spain.

Cheating in sport, especially the use of drugs for advantage, has grown for two reasons: the adversarial mind-set of many athletes — athletes with the attitude that they must win at all costs — and professionalism, that is, money. Contracts in many sports are worth millions to the top athletes, which is a huge driving force to take banned substances. Every athlete knows what substances are banned in their sport, or they should. 'I didn't know' is no excuse in any sport.

However, the science of sports physiology and pharmacology is advancing at such a fast rate that many drugs athletes are using have yet to be identified or banned. It's still cheating though, and any cheating at any time is a major withdrawal from your integrity account.

POSITIVE ROLE MODELS FOR KIDS

In a similar vein to cheating is the 'angry spectator' situation that seems to have become more common these days. These are the parents, coaches or spectators who stand on the sidelines and very vocally provide a negative commentary on the game. These are the parents screaming at the kids to try harder, not for the individual's performance, but to beat the other team, to satisfy *their* need to win at all costs. These are the spectators or coaches that abuse the referees on the field, both vocally and occasionally physically, because they perceive 'injustices'. I regard these manifestations of sport in the same way as the negative competition culture and consider them equally as unpalatable as cheating.

We all have the responsibility to provide our youth with positive role models — in sport, business and at home — to instil in them the culture of personal responsibility and achievement.

A PERSONAL ACHIEVEMENT

In January of 2002 I was put in the unenviable position of defending myself against claims of cheating after my climb of Aoraki/Mount Cook. After the Christmas attempt petered out at about 3100 metres, when I returned to finish the climb I flew in to the Bowie Corner on the Linda Glacier at about 2800 metres or so. I was going back to complete what I had started and to finish the documentary that Chas Toogood was filming. I climbed from there, missing out four or five hours of non-technical trudging up the glacier. After the summiting the film crew and I flew off the mountain just above the summit rocks — possibly a rash decision, but done. Many have criticised me for that, claiming that I cheated — cheated them perhaps but not myself. I did the climb for myself, for my desire to stand again on the summit of Mount Cook, to prove the leg design that Wayne had created for me — not to be the first double amputee to climb Mount Cook. In fact, I have never formally claimed the ascent. I will the day I climb it from bottom to top — a feat which less than 30 percent of the climbers that claim the summit achieve.

For me that climb and the criticism that it generated in a few people (many of whom don't consider climbing a sport) made me look hard at my integrity account. I consider that I made a big deposit that day, not a withdrawal.

> ## SUMMARY PANEL
> ### Race yourself
>
> - *Achievement-based sport releases your potential.*
> - *Racing yourself is the key to real success.*
> - *Be open about the definition of sport, it doesn't always have to involve beating someone else.*
> - *Even in 'opponent' sports, the 'race yourself' philosophy holds true.*
> - *Great teams in sport and business are based on the concept of personal responsibility, respect, and free communication.*
> - *Kids need positive sports role models; don't be the angry spectator.*
> - *Your integrity account is just as important in sport as in the rest of your life.*

17. In the zone, but what zone?

The concept of 'zone' is used within many differing sports, businesses and cultures, but the core element remains the same – the concept of being in a defined space or condition. Even in sport 'the zone' can mean many things. It has connotations of an actual place (above 8000 metres — the death zone), a diet (the 60 percent carbohydrate, 20 percent protein and 20 percent fats diet of Dr Barry Sears) and of course the most common zone concept, the performance 'zone' — an ideal state that is the primary focus of elite athletes.

WHERE IS THE ZONE?
Have you ever been in the zone? You don't need to be an elite athlete to experience the mental state it represents. Think of a time where whatever you were doing — be it cooking, computer programming, driving, fishing, dealing with a client, or perhaps even doing your accounts —

completing the task felt effortless. Think back to a situation where you felt in charge, powerful and graceful, completely relaxed, your mind clear, totally on the task at hand. If you have ever felt like this then you were in the zone.

Being in the zone is critical to elite athletes. Sprinters, swimmers, golfers — in fact every individual sport — all rely on years of training imprinting the perfect movements for that sport to such a level they become automatic. Sprinters need to focus on a balance between style and effort. The effort they need to make is extreme, but that effort is wasted if it isn't effectively turned into speed. Often the difference between a winning time and second place is mere hundredths of a second. Not the amount of effort or commitment but an infinitesimal efficiency advantage to the winner.

I have had several clear experiences of being in the zone myself. Each time the experience of being in the zone has manifested itself in a self-belief that has allowed me to perform. Although in each case, after completing the task or the event I knew exactly what mistakes I had made and how to perform it better next time.

EXPERIENCING THE ZONE MOMENT

Take for example, my 'kilo' (1000-metre individual time trial) ride at the Sydney Paralympics. Before heading to Sydney, as I have mentioned before, the road race was going to be my forte. The kilo was something I had physiologically trained for, but the skill and experience of riding on an international-level wooden velodrome was something completely outside my experience.

In fact, arriving in Sydney in early October, my lack of experience was clearly evident. The first day on the extremely steep velodrome was a real challenge. I must have done 10 laps on the flat 'neutral' area before gathering the courage to go up onto the steep wooden racing line. I even needed to be educated on where I could ride — the 'road rules' of track racing — essential when your bike doesn't have brakes and has a 'fixed' back wheel, meaning no freewheeling or sudden speed changes. I very rapidly realised though, that with a bit of practice the skills would become a non-issue, to the extent that by race day I knew I had a real chance of performing at medal level.

During the 10 minutes before I stepped onto my bike I knew that I had definitely found 'the zone'. Everything felt as though it was in slow motion: I could feel every fibre, every pulse in my body, and each message transmitted 'we're ready'. Normally before a race my base heart rate will rise to over 100 bpm with nervous tension, but before I warmed up (on my road bike set up on a windtrainer), my heart rate was only 63 bpm, barely above my resting rate. I was thinking about the moment, not about the past or the future, but just the upcoming one and a half minutes.

After riding to a silver medal in my kilo — and even before all the other riders had completed their ride — I knew the few elements that I could do better. The elements I would have to fix, otherwise if I was once again put in that situation I wouldn't be in the zone. Elitism is all about striving for that kind of perfection. Training all the components of an event, how they go together, perfecting them, analysing the weaknesses and working on them. All so that the next time you are in the situation you can again enter the zone.

Because of my tendency to strive for perfection I often find it hard to repeatedly enter the zone in some events. After tasting how good it was, I need it to be better next time, which entails greater commitment — the subsequent performance needs to be to the next level.

When you aren't in the zone, you really have set yourself up for a difficult time, especially if you have set your expectations well above your training. If you aren't in the zone then it is likely that the requisite perfection of action, of movement or thinking isn't going to happen, automatically putting you at a disadvantage.

TRAINING FOR THE ZONE
So how do you find your way into the zone? Number one entry criterion is to do the work beforehand, to train those actions and for that event. An effort without training is essentially cheating yourself. Also, the zone depends on the situation or the outcome of the event being reliant on

your performance, on the combination of your skill and effort. Don't expect to enter the zone when you are trying to choose your Lotto numbers or the winning ticket of a raffle. Once you have the training sussed, entering the zone becomes an exercise in self-belief and relaxation, a balance between being sharp on the day without being overstressed.

For me, in the lead-up to an event, I have learned to spend the final week concentrating on relaxation, tapering and refreshing both mentally and physiologically. Even more importantly, the closer to the event, the less I think about what's been and what's to come. Unless you have a chronically short memory, the weeks beforehand were the time to be concentrating on the race plan. Now is the time to be living in the present, feeling the good vibes, assessing how calm and strong you are.

Race day is all about concentrating on the task at hand. In the days immediately before and especially on 'race' day (be it on the bike, skis, climbing or presenting) I am very focused, in fact very selfish. I rely on inner strength for focus — external interruptions just distract me (hence the family head for the hills). That level of 'self' is vital once the event starts, because then it is your strength, focus and skill which determine the outcome. This is also the reason and the time to practise the 'race yourself' mentality.

AIM FOR THE ZONE

As a young climber I used to revel in the zone. I would feel like I was in a protective bubble, executing clear, firm, fluid movements, seeing the immediate environment, living in the moment. Since becoming an amputee I never really found that same zone until January 2002 on the summit ice cap of Mount Cook/Aoraki. There the urge to run up the steep hard ice was difficult to curb, I was feeling that good.

However, a very real focus of the zone concept in climbing is the place known as the 'death zone'. This is any place over 8000 metres where the human body is in an alien environment. If you were placed on top of Mount Everest at 8848 metres without first acclimatising then you would be unlikely to live more than 20 minutes due to a lack of oxygen. Even when acclimatised and with supplementary oxygen, your body and mind deteriorate at a rapid rate. Even at 7600 metres on the North or South Cols, any longer than three days results in a body that is lucky to make it down, let alone up. Equally insidiously, the lack of oxygen results in impaired thinking and poor rationalisation, increasing the risk of death — this is life in the death zone.

No matter what we do, to achieve the best result, to aim for the perfect 'game', it's essential that we strive to enter the zone, the place where our individual potential has the best chance of being expressed.

> ## SUMMARY PANEL
> ### In the zone, but what zone?
>
> - *The zone can be found everywhere — in sport, business and life.*
> - *The zone can be a physical place (like the death zone or a diet) or a mental attitude.*
> - *The zone is about living in the moment.*
> - *The zone occurs once you get every other facet of the event under control including training and skills.*
> - *The zone is like being in an energy flow or capsule where you are in total control.*
> - *The zone is the place where your potential finds its best chance of being expressed.*

18. Visualisation: seeing it happen, making it happen

I bet any athlete 30 years ago who confessed to making use of visualisation would have been branded a dreamer; even today there are plenty of cynics around.

THE THREE ELEMENTS OF VISUALISATION
I consider the skill of visualisation to be intimately linked to three things:

- Self-confidence and self-belief
- Previous experience of the environment or situation
- Having put in the necessary training so you have no negative thoughts or regrets once you step up to the start line.

The ability to see in your mind's eye an action or outcome is a double-edged sword. The essence of visualisation, which is to picture the positive elements of what you want to do, is not necessarily as easy as you might think. Just sitting here now, focus on some action — be it riding a hill, running a race, or perhaps giving a presentation to the board. Almost invariably some level of negative thought will creep in. Watch any elite sport, observe the athletes in the starting gate or blocks, you can see them visualising the race. Often the biggest difference in performance between them is that some will be losing the race right there and then, as they let negative images intrude.

VISUALISATION IN ACTION

The Paralympics at Sydney in 2000 taught me more about visualisation than probably any other experience in my short life. In fact, I wish I had known enough about the skill to use it positively all those years ago when I first had my legs off.

I was entered into two races in Sydney: the 'kilo', a 1000-metre individual time trial on the 250-metre banked track in the Dunc Gray Velodrome, which I referred to in the previous chapter; and the 50-km road race for my class, LC3 (the class for athletes with one leg off above the knee or both legs off below the knee).

As I mentioned, before heading to Sydney I had no experience at all on the steeply banked wooden tracks used in international track racing. I can assure you, any visualisation I did on those first few days had more to do with the damage I would do to myself, my carbon cycling legs and my pride by falling off, than 'dreams' of success in the velodrome. The road race was a different kettle of fish though. All the information had shown a big hill on the course — perfect for me. I was going to sleep every night dreaming of blowing the race apart and grabbing an unassailable lead sprinting up that hill — that's what I had trained my heart out to do and was getting damn good at as well. The reality, as it turned out, was miles different.

After five days of training at the velodrome I was confident that I had done the work to do well. Perhaps not to 'win', but that's not what I was aiming for. After the first day on that track I knew I could do very well, and possibly better than I had ever hoped with my lack of experience of that type of riding. By the third day it wasn't winning the kilo I wanted but a tilt at the world record. In training I had ridden the two components of the kilo (the start lap, to practise getting off the line, and a 'flying' three-lap circuit) in times that would come close to a new world record. All I had to do on the day was put it all together.

However, on that start line I was not visualising winning, not visualising breaking the world record (which stood at just over one minute and 21 seconds), but visualising the perfect start and the perfect last three laps. I knew from those preceding days of work what I needed to do, I knew from the months of training that a good race was in the legs, and I had few regrets — I *knew* I could do a race that I would be proud of.

From the start to the finish I was focused on doing the job. Even as the one minute and 23 seconds unfolded I maintained the concentration — it felt like hours. As I crossed the finish line I knew that the time was good — I knew that I had given it everything. The feeling was like a restrained elation — you don't want to hope too much until you can look up, get the eyes focused and see the time clock: 1:23 it read, fastest so far — yee ha!

For me that race was almost a self-fulfilling prophecy: visualise the right actions, think the right thoughts, do the right work and the result will be what you deserve; in this case the silver medal.

Now the road race was equally a lesson in visualisation, but it was a very negative mental video I ended up playing to myself. Once again it was an example of a self-fulfilling prophecy, although this time to my detriment.

Why? Well the buggers took the hill out, that's why. The race course originally had a big steep hill in it, the same as the Olympic course — perfect for me as hill climbing on the bike is my strength. So my months of training and visualising hammering up the Bronte Beach hill evaporated. The nearest thing to a hill that I had left to play with was a 300-metre-long hump in Centennial Park; too far from the finish to be of any good to me at all. My positive mental imagery became quite negative, and while I tried to push the negative thoughts away I didn't have the skills to manage it or the confidence (or too big an ego) to talk to anyone about it. By the time I lined up on the start line the most prominent thought I had was, 'Let's get this over and done with, now.'

With sprinting ability and obvious fitness I became a 'marked man' in the peleton. No one could catch me up that hill; I led up it with 20 metres to spare and gas in the tank on each lap but they came thundering past 500 metres later. With the exception of that time on the 'hill' I spent the rest of the race talking myself out of the win. This was a case of having done the work, of having some good road race experience behind me, but lacking that third element, the self-confidence to put it all together.

ELIMINATE NEGATIVE IMAGES

So what do you do if those negative thoughts start to dominate? Well, if you haven't done the work then either head home or else ensure that your expectations mirror your work. No, I don't mean talk yourself down. Don't limit your potential, don't put a lid on what you can achieve, but approach the event as a learning experience, a training race perhaps. Once you have the appropriate attitude to the race or event, then try and let any negative images and thoughts drift away; just ignore them so they get smaller and smaller in the periphery of your perception, further away from you and your desired image. Don't try and change them as that just refocuses and ingrains them.

At the same time, enhance a positive. Your mind isn't like a television screen where someone else chooses the programme you are to see. It's more like your own personal digital video edit suite. You can focus on whatever you like, make it whatever size or colour you like, but just make sure you do it. Use it because it is a skill that needs practice — the more you do it the better at visualisation you get.

Take a skill sport like skiing for instance. Learn how a ski works in a turn, then use that knowledge to become a micro camera in the base watching the snow crystals flash by blindingly fast; imagine the perfect dynamic turn — left then right, get some air, left again — easy and cool isn't it?

Perhaps I'm a bit of a slow learner because climbing Aoraki/Mount Cook as a double amputee was another exercise in visualisation, both negative and positive. The unsuccessful climb in December 2001 was just like the Paralympic road race, a classic case of a negative self-fulfilling prophecy if ever there was one. So how, if I have supposedly learned all these lessons, did it come about? Easy — I took my 'eye off the ball', a real crime when you need to be focused to perform; especially in mountaineering where that lack of focus tends to bite you in the butt. Once again it was a change in circumstance that did the damage, just like losing the big hill and my projected advantage at the Paralympics.

In the months leading up to the climb I was visualising (or perhaps dreaming) of being there; of climbing hard snow and ice on the steep Linda shelf; of doing the two pitches of exposed technical rock and ice that make up the Summit Rocks; and of front pointing up the majestic summit ice cap to stand once again on Aoraki. I spent those months studying everything that might go wrong, focusing on and practising all the techniques and decision making around fixing broken prosthetic feet, crampons, sockets and other hardware. Ensuring that I was carrying the minimum to survive if storms caught me. Ensuring I was familiar with modern abseil and lowering techniques; even how to turn a snow shovel into a sled in the event one or both of my prosthetic limbs failed. I knew there was a chance that it would be my stumps that might pose problems, but I didn't have enough experience of what it would be like (stump-wise) so couldn't effectively prepare. In fact, I thought I could walk through any pain, having experienced some 'gold standards' of pain already.

In the last few days, negative images started to erode some of my self-confidence — not so much with regard to my ability but more about the consequences of failure. The ownership of this goal had grown to belong to more than just the climbing team, my family and myself, it had become public property. Consequently I (wrongly) felt a huge responsibility to climb the sucker in the allocated time.

More negative images intruded when several days before climbing we flew into the Plateau and onto the Tasman Glacier. The snow was soft and wet, I was slipping and sliding all over the place, the legs totally unsuited to soft conditions. Stepping onto the Plateau several days later just eroded the confidence even further. While looking up at the summit, heaps of positive images of the technical climbing flooded in, but always in the background was the image — like a screen saver on my mental PC — of the frustration of moving up the lower slopes in soft conditions.

As it turned out, I climbed in those soft conditions, and nothing broke. Nothing that is, except my body: too little fuel, too long between rests, and too hard on the stumps.

I spent the next three weeks at home recovering and training, spending a lot of time on positive visualisation: both of outcome, technique and strategies for coping with the 'curve balls' I seem to attract. I mentally ticked off those three elements again:

- Self-belief: I knew even more clearly now that I could do it — all I had to do was ensure the others understood my climbing style and abilities so this time I could stamp my style on the climb with confidence;
- Previous experience of the environment or situation: I now had this, which built even more confidence — I knew I could meet every challenge given the next step;
- Having done the work, having no regrets: having found new strategies to cope with stump damage and climbing style and even more training — I was fully prepared.

Focus, single-mindedness, call it what you like, it sure made the difference the second time.

FROM VISION TO REALITY

You can use visualisation to better express your potential at every level. Try it in some of these situations and see if it helps.

- You are climbing a decent hill during a race or a bunch ride; up in front there is the slowly disappearing back of another rider. Imagine an elastic cord is stretched tight between you. Focus on their butt and that cord and feel it draw you to them.
- You just don't feel like going out to train? No particular reason, just down in the dumps, a bit tired, legs feel dead? Drag yourself out and put your mind into visualisation mode. Don't think about being next world champion (unless your ego demands it), just focus on one aspect of your gait — your pedal stroke perhaps. If you are out on the bike, do every turn (make some curves if the road or track is straight) as perfectly as possible: outside pedal down with all your weight on it, lean that bike. I visualise myself on skis, the perfect bike turn feels just the same, especially if you can feel the energy flowing through you via the skis or the bike and into the ground, forming an imaginary railroad track. Perhaps you are doing some hill training for the next running race, transport yourself to the mountains of Nepal — just imagine you are running the steep, high-altitude tracks that reach up towards the majestic peaks — train there and you will succeed anywhere!
- Use sound, either the right music to inspire you, or sounds that you make yourself. Watch the track cycling stars or weightlifters. They often spend time visualising exactly the critical few seconds with headphones on, and when they execute the actions they vocalise them as well — everything from grunts and screams to their own personal mantras. I find this technique hugely powerful in lots of

situations — in a kilo or a sprint, the first few critical pedal strokes are accompanied (and timed) with a powerful, 'YES, YES, YES!' For me it helps focus all the energy that my little engine can produce through my legs and into the bike. Then I change to a lower intensity, faster-timed mantra, frequently, 'you can do it, you can do it, you can do it, you can do it'.

- Try visualisation on longer events as well. The Rainbow Rage is a 106-km mountain bike adventure ride/race I regularly participate in. I've had some good rides and some terrible rides, the times all within 10 percent of each other — the difference was all to do with the stress, expectation and visualisation before and during each. Check out Chapter 19 for the two rides; on the best one I sang to myself the whole way (I'd scare the wildlife if I ever sang out loud), 'I feel good, da, da, da', over and over again. And I did.
- Watch rock climbers, they play a mental video of each move, linking them together in their minds, just like ballet dancers. They practise all the individual moves before putting them together to 'redpoint' the route — that is, doing it all in one fluid climb.

Visualisation is just as important in business, and essential where the boundaries of business and art merge. It is an extension of the 'dream', a pre-production of the event or product in the mind of its creator. John Britten, the innovative engineer and entrepreneur who created perhaps the world's most exclusive and innovative motorbike, the Britten V1000, always considered his 'gift', his greatest advantage in business, to be his ability to see the final product in his mind's eye. He then worked backwards to make it a reality. The final look of the first V1000 was created using wire and a hot-glue gun, building the external form before even laying the first sheets of carbon fibre.

So use visualisation — use it every day, in every way. It's a tool that'll help you grow, that will help those big dreams become a reality.

> ## SUMMARY PANEL
> ### Visualisation
>
> - *Tick off the three elements — self-confidence, previous experience and 'no regrets'.*
> - *Let negative images drift away and fade, filling the void with positive images.*
> - *Use your mind as your own video edit suite to manufacture exciting, skilled and positive images.*
> - *Use sounds, external and internal, to reinforce the visual images.*

Section Four

Mark's passions

So often in this book I have talked about the importance of passion and commitment, the importance of having a 'must do' attitude. I have learned these lessons through my passion for cycling, mountaineering and food. Here I take the opportunity to explain what is special about each of these passions, and I hope it will give you a greater insight into why they have had such a formative influence on my life.

19. The culture of the bike: the last hard sport?

Lance Armstrong, five times winner of the Tour de France and cancer survivor, called his autobiography *It's Not About the Bike*. I guess what he's trying to convey in that title is that, independent of his cancer, cycling is about a culture of challenge and competition. At its highest levels it's also a lucrative profession with all the attendant problems that come with multi-million dollar salaries (i.e. drug cheats). But hey, even at my level, on the fringes of international competition, and even at a local level, the culture of cycling is as intense as any international professional sport.

CYCLING CULTURE
Cycling grows on you, in fact many of us find it addictive, and like climbing it can act as an anchor or cornerstone to your life. Not because of the obvious technology (even though for a gear freak like me, it just

makes it more fun and addictive), but because of the challenge, risk (to your mind/ego and body) and the attendant feelings of achievement which come with that.

As an example, Jeremy my son, a talented 18-year-old, recently competed in a gruelling mountain bike race of over 100 km. Jerry thought he had a good chance to do well in his age group, under 19s; he had raced the course three times before, knew what to expect, and had always made it in times which showed what an elite athlete he is. This year was a disaster, however. He went into the race a bit tired, having had a series of low-level chronic health problems and knee trouble; added to long hours in a new career, he set himself up for a bad day — and what a bad day he had.

I was tired from being on the road doing presentations for two weeks, so had given the race a miss as it's not the kind of race to go into tired. Standing at the finish line waiting for him I became increasingly worried. Once the time went over five hours I knew what he would be feeling and thinking. Some of the racers I knew came past, and they said he looked terrible, was feeling sick and his knees were playing up. As soon as I saw him coming into the finish zone I made sure I was there to grab him — he wasn't too steady on his feet, let alone the bike. I shepherded him straight over to the car, put him in the front seat with a drink, threw the bike on the back and got him out of there, straight home to a hot shower.

Cycling is such a hard sport that when you have such a bad day, if you don't get on top of it quickly then it'll suck your motivation away, suck you dry. After a shower and getting some food and drink, the resilience of youth took over. He had his body and head straight again — I wish my own ageing body and mind recovered that well.

However, the point of the whole story, besides describing how hard a sport like cycling can be, is how others saw Jerry's performance and interpreted our comments about it. People would ask, 'How did Jeremy go?' I'd reply, 'Terrible, he really sucked, with probably his worst day on a bike.' Immediately they would come straight back at me with, 'That's a bit mean, I'm sure he tried hard.' What they didn't understand was that the last thing he wanted was any sort of ill-informed sympathy.

This was an experience to salvage some valuable lessons from and promptly put behind him.

SOME CYCLING FACTS

The modern bike is a technologically advanced and complex machine, but it is still just a tool for the job. Competitive cycling these days can be divided up into road, track, mountain and BMX racing. Within each of these divisions there are all the classes. For instance, mountain biking is divided into cross country, downhill, trials, freeride, dual slalom, endurance (24-hr), and more to be invented I'm sure. Road cycling is traditionally split into time trials, criteriums, one-day races and multi-stage tours. Track cycling has a multitude of race types such as the kilo (1000-metre individual time trial), the pursuit (4000 metres against the clock or another rider), sprint, Olympic sprint and points race, to name a few. BMX is raced on closed dirt tracks on small-wheeled single-speed bikes; often considered a kids' activity, it is in fact not just the proving ground for some excellent riders but a multi-million dollar sport in its own right.

CYCLING TERMINOLOGY

Blow Like runners 'hitting the wall', going out too fast, too hard and running out of energy and strength, frequently only able to crawl home. Also called 'bonk'.

Break One or more riders who escape off a group in the race.

Bridge To join the group (break) out in front. Almost always a tactical move or else you end up pulling the whole group up to the break and lose the advantage.

Cadence Pedal stroke measured in revolutions per minute, that is, how quickly you are pedalling.

Domestique Team rider who sacrifices his chances of success for that of a team-mate. Damn hard to do sometimes.

Echelon Staggered formation of riders in a crosswind.

GC General Classification, the overall placing in a race, especially muti-stage tours.

Hook Occurs in two ways. One is when you are riding very close to another rider and their handlebars lock under yours. As they struggle for control they lift your front wheel off the ground — only one way to go then and that's down. The other, common even in the professional peleton, is when a back wheel rubs against another rider's front wheel — once again you go down. An illegal, aggressive and dirty tactic sometimes used deliberately in road races.

HRM Heart rate monitor. Used to assess how hard you are working and how well you are recovering.

Jump No, not off the ground, but a quick burst of speed, used to break away from a group. You 'jump' out of the saddle, sprinting to surprise others.

Kick That final burst of speed when you are maxed out.

Lactic acid A product of the body's metabolism. As we exercise the level increases from a resting one millimole (the scientific measure of the acid) per litre to about four. Over four cannot be sustained — it's the burn we feel in our muscles when we push ourselves to the limit.

Peleton The main group of cyclists during a race or bunch ride. The strongest teams control the race through controlling the peleton, determining the pace and controlling groups that escape off the front.

Pull To ride at the front into the wind — the hardest place to ride.

Pursuit 3000-metre to 4000-metre time trial, with two riders on the track at once. They start on opposite straights, and the fastest time wins; although if one rider catches and passes the other, then the race is won right there.

Reps Repetitions of very intense but brief training elements to simulate the intensity of racing. Used also in weight training. Typical would be 5 minutes at 90 percent max, 6 minutes recovery, or perhaps 1 min 30s, four of them as hard as possible, 10 minutes in between to recover.

Sit-in To rest in someone's draught, not pulling or working (you'll get hooked if you do it too much).

Spin To pedal fluidly and quickly — a great way to ride as it spreads all the forces. The sign of an experienced rider (the opposite is a 'masher' who strains away pushing a large gear at a low cadence).
Toast Fried, burnt, cooked; comes after blowing and bonking — not pretty.
Velodrome The track for cycle racing. Usually a 250-metre oval shape with steep ends (up to 52 degrees) and two short straights (also sloping, at about 12 degrees). The track surface is either concrete (outdoor) or wooden (indoor).

To train for all these events takes a huge commitment, both in the short term (20 hours per week-plus frequently) and in the long term, as the training effect is cumulative — meaning that you get better every year, that you can train to a more intensive degree each succeeding year (that is, until age catches up). Even a race like the kilo, just 1000 metres, takes training that involves hundreds of kilometres per week for months and years on end, as well as intensive gym work.

The other aspect of all these types of competitive cycling is that in each discipline you can just back off and stop at any time — unlike mountaineering, ocean rowing and other completely committing sports, where if you stop you may die. Strange as it may sound, to me that makes it even harder, as the urge to achieve, the desire to push yourself, to subject your body to extreme pain, has to come from within. I always joke that the kilo would be far easier if you didn't have a brain. There is no strategy other than to go as hard as you possibly can from the start, then some more.

Here are a couple of my own experiences of cycling in its many forms to explain what I mean.

THE RACE FROM HELL

March 12: grapes coming out of my ears, the yard of the winery is full to overflowing — some well-intentioned person filled every 400-kg box God invented. The tarmac outside the winery's press room has 205 boxes of premium grapes (well, at least every box the winery owned), and I have a group of barely experienced staff and a long, long night ahead. What has this got to do with the race from hell? Well, it was the situation that turned a great idea into a hellish event.

Vintage had as usual started with a vengeance a week earlier with grapes for Deutz coming in through the gate. But it had really started weeks earlier with the constant rounds of the vineyards, tasting grapes to determine quality, collecting samples, analysing data, estimating crop levels — all those things which consume a winemaker's every waking hour. Unfortunately I was supposed to be riding as well, training for the 106-km mountain bike adventure race, the Rainbow Rage. Now if I possessed the correct quota of brains I wouldn't have even contemplated doing both, but some stubborn streak in me kicked in and said, 'I really want to do this and I don't see why making wine should interfere with my life to that extent — I make so many sacrifices that this is one too many.' Actually it was probably the time, if not the day that I decided that wine was taking away too much of life and life's opportunities. The seven-year itch to try something different had struck again.

The race was on Saturday the 14th — no chance of any reprieve before it either, as those grapes just don't stop. Planning, writing job instructions, teaching staff, worrying continuously that every member of the team would not so much perform, but that they wouldn't cock everything up. I'll tell you what, every day arriving at work during vintage I'd cringe — walking in the door of the winemaker's office would lift the blood pressure 30 points at least in anticipation of hearing about a cock-up. It didn't matter if it was mine or someone else's — grapes ruined or juice down the drain hurt like a punch in the guts. That's what passion costs.

March 13: grapes dominate, people and crises complicate the day. I needed to be home by 8 pm to pack and get some kind of sleep, but working every day from 10 am to 2 or 3 am has ingrained the sleep patterns. Scrape home at 9 pm, still with zillions of thoughts, zillions of tasks cruising the brain. I sleep fitfully, tossing and turning, dreaming of stuff-ups I might have made. Six am comes too soon; I crawl out of bed and try and eat some food but all I feel is sick. I hate being late, so I spend the next 30 minutes hunting everyone out of the house and into the car, continually checking that we have everything.

Once on the road you'd think things would calm down, but no, I try to eat again and just about throw up the muesli bar, or at least the half I managed to choke down. It was going to be a bloody long day.

Start area was the usual bedlam: 1400 people had turned up, cars, campers, vans and buses all shoehorned into a boulder-strewn field. The loos had a queue a mile long, so off into the bush to have a pee. Double-check all the gear again and it's time to try and get a starting position. With 1400 mountain bikers you don't want to be anywhere but up near the front. The back makers (those cyclists happy to cruise along at the back) will take probably 10 to 15 minutes to get across the start line and you have no choice about a group to ride with — if you are at the back at the start then you are playing catch-up all day. I managed to position the bike about 20 places from the front. I knew that probably almost 700 or so riders would pass me in the first 20 kilometres, but I'd pass lots on the big hill — that's life.

Just standing and leaning on the bike for the 40 minutes until the gun was the nearest thing to rest I'd had for weeks. I felt flat, tired and on edge. People were constantly wanting to strike up conversation but I just didn't have it in me. I tried to be pleasant but it was a struggle, 'avoid eye contact at all costs so they don't get an invite to speak'.

The start gun was a relief. The race is always neutralised for the first five km — that is, there is a pace car that keeps everyone at about 30 km/h so the 1400 riders can stretch out along the road, minimising, but not eliminating, the carnage associated with that many riders in one group. You have to be sharp, most of these guys have never ridden in a peleton, don't understand any of the rules and have little skill and awareness. Someone goes down right in front of me in the first 300 metres, I dodge off the road, stay upright and fight for a place back on the seal. I'm trying to keep at least a bike-length clear in front of my front wheel, any more and some sod slots in and I have to brake. After 10 km I feel as though everyone has passed me, my heart rate is up at 85 percent and I'm going 20 percent slower than even the fat boys and old men. Shit it's going to be a long way.

At 17 km the seal gives way to dirt road; down a steep rutted and rocky hill, two sharp hairpin turns and a gnarly ford through a cold swift stream. Well, everyone that passed me is right there, the scene looks like a Discovery channel programme on wildebeest crossing the Zambesi. At least 30 riders are blocking the entrance to the ford; no choice but to get off and struggle through the rocky streambed to one side. There are people up-ended everywhere.

The track out was steep, needing the lowest gear and a bit of elbow room; but worse for me, nowhere to start off from. Without the fine feel of feet, clipping in is difficult; I really need two bike-lengths of flat area or something to lean against — neither was available there. After stuffing around for a few minutes, getting jostled by the crowd, I pushed the bike up the first steep section a few hundred metres until I found a tree to use: on and away. Starting to feel not too bad actually, heart rate still too high but not getting worse, drinking OK and nibbling at a few bars. The day might turn out alright after all.

No, wrong again. As I came out of the tree-lined rocky gorge into the open high valleys, the track started to head up along with my heart rate. Speed went down and I was feeling sick. At 45 km the first big hill, and it shattered me. Crawling over the top in the wee gears, people were still passing me. It wasn't right, I always catch people up here, but not today.

A long downhill and then the road started up another alpine valley. By this time the sun was taking its toll, 30°C and a slight tailwind, can't actually drink enough to keep up with the sweating. Then that dreaded noise, 'pist, pist, pist'. Air leaking out of the front tyre with every revolution. Punctures are a nightmare, the race tyres are so hard to get off; I can't stand and balance so have to sit, and I just don't have the energy. I hate stopping. When I start again I need to readjust the legs, the stump socks and sockets and my arse — almost better to keep riding. God I hate these pissy-arsed little pumps, it takes ages; my forearms are cramping, not a good sign.

Back on the bike, five km to go until the big hill. I start to get a bit of rhythm and then cramp hits me in the right hamstring. Aaagh, no! Not cramp! Spin it out, lower the power going through the pedals, drink some more. Christ, not cramp before the hill! Try and eat a bar but it comes straight back up, barfing up valuable fluid and fuel.

I must ride the hill, it's 500 metres of vertical climbing, steep rocky track. If I stop on it then I'll be unlikely to get going again and will have to walk up the bloody thing in the cycling legs, not a pretty thought at all. I always ride this hill, at least half the riders will walk it so it's a matter of pride, it's about showing ability.

Weaving up that scorching track, the slopes all around chock-full of blue borage and rosehip in flower — and unfortunately all the bumble-bees that pollinate them. I'm wearing blue and seem to attract every one of them so the inevitable finally happens, my 20 km/h and Mister Bee's 20 km/h speeds result in a 40 km/h head-on with my chest. I could feel the sting immediately and the swelling start. I'm not normally allergic to bees but with the day I was having it had to happen. It looked like I was growing a breast in the middle of my chest it was swelling so quick. It made me feel sick, even sicker as I came around the last flat turn and could look all the way up that hill. The riders going over the top looked like worker ants from where I was.

What a nightmare, it went on and on. Walkers wouldn't get out of the way, almost putting me off the road several times; I resented the hell out of them, I resented having to use valuable air to ask them to move. Twenty minutes of thinking small, thinking the next corner, just keep going until the next corner, then the next, then the one after that.

Over the top, 100 or so riders resting, filling drink bottles at an aid station. Why rest before going down? I can never understand it — you've just climbed a monster hill and it is 46 km of mostly downhill and flat home — surely no time to be resting.

The downhill is hairy — deep gravel between two rocky wheel tracks, deep water table on the left, very steep drop down hundreds of metres on the right. I always scare myself here and today even worse, overshooting a corner and careering off into the water table, almost hitting the ground. Slow down and survive became the plan for the rest of the hill.

Then that bloody sound again — I couldn't believe it, another puncture! I never get punctures, so two in one day? Fitted the last tube, I always carry two and some patches as well, and started off again. The road was so rutted that in places I couldn't pedal, the legs would keep stalling. I knew there were at least 30 km of ruts to go. I was just about crying, I was swearing and cursing. Everyone was riding right by. How could there still be people behind me? I was sure they must have all passed me ages ago.

The hours are ticking by; five hours gone and I'm still one hill from the finish line. Smooth road signalled 13 km to go, up the steady last climb, going OK as long as I keep spinning. Try for a bit of power and cramp returns and the stomach revolts. Eight km to go, all downhill, just stay on. Vision is blurred, starting to see dots, seeing stars, just hang on. 'Pist, pist, pist' — no, not another puncture! Bugger it, I'll ride the flat, who cares if I stuff the tyre and the rim? I have to do less than six hours and if I stop I'll go over for sure: besides, no tube to use, only patches. If it was hairy before it's worse now; the front is skittering and slithering all over the place, threatening to dump me on my nose every other second.

The last 300 metres, people lining the road yelling encouragement, the last damn thing I want to hear. My performance has been so poor, I want the earth to open up and swallow me. At the finish line the nightmare continues. I cross, keeping on riding until I'm away from everyone, and then just drop to the ground. Tears of frustration, pain, disappointment, well up — I just need to get the hell out of there. The post-race inquisition that always occurs makes me want to puke. I know what I did wrong. I know every second of that race and want to relive no part of it for anyone.

It wasn't the Tour de France, it wasn't the Olympics, it wasn't a matter of life or death, so why the hell did I put myself through such a humiliating and shitty day? That I don't know, but it was probably due to a mixture of being too proud, too dumb, too blind, too greedy, too possessed and too obsessed.

Lessons to be learned? None right then — it was just too close and painful. The lesson came afterwards.

RIDE, NOT RACE

Two years later: March 13 this time. The yard is still full of grapes, my last vintage. The passion has dimmed, still there but it has sucked so much out of me that I had to say stop, no more. Still training, still cajoling and trying to motivate people to share the dream, release the potential in those grapes. The difference is I can see an end now, but more importantly I can see a new beginning.

The difference this time is that I have some space in life. I haven't written the jobs, I've told people what they need to do. Shared the responsibility around perfectly capable people, people that have the knowledge and the information, so I don't have to worry. Wish I'd had them around me a year ago.

Home in plenty of time to pack the car, check out the bikes and the gear, get everything packed while not feeling a hint of stress. Even better, getting home so early meant cooking a nice dinner — a real treat during vintage when every meal is either cooked like a zombie or too rushed to count. A decent sleep, up in plenty of time and even food in the stomach. Things were going pretty well — amazing what eight hours of real, unworried sleep does for you.

The difference this time around was in the anticipation of the event, rather than resentment of work for making the event such a difficult task.

Why sit on the start line for 40 minutes when you are going to ride for five-plus hours! I got there, watched the hordes milling around, and decided to be a hard-nosed bugger like others. I took my bike up to about 50 metres back from the start, an area already full of keen, hyped bikers. I just stood the bike up and said, 'I'll be back soon, just have to work on the legs' — it worked a treat.

I went and sat in the back of the truck until 10 minutes before the start. Then I wandered across, picked up the bike and shouldered my way into the queue; a few apologies and a few dirty looks but tough, I'm just taking disabled parking privileges to a new level.

The start gun as usual means five km of neutralised cruising, avoiding the less than experienced riders, lots of them freaking out in the crush, falling over everywhere. This seems somewhat repetitive, I think.

It's a bit like slalom ski racing really, dodging the fallen riders, the slow weaving ones, just like attacking a steep run. Weight on the outside ski (pedal), carve around them, flick the weight to the other side, and carve around another. A big grin plastered on the face — this is fun!

The difference? I was racing myself, no one else, nothing to prove to anyone other than myself. There was no one in that whole ride that was my competitor other than me. Bugger the lot of them. So many people would come up and say how well I would do against people with legs — I think not.

Once again I'm with over 1000 riders, heading over that same 106 km of rocky trail and big hills. As usual, hundreds power past me; I chat, say hi, good luck, what a fantastic day, nice bike, nice legs — you know just the usual cyclist chatter.

Cruising at 80 percent heart rate through the beech forest, only a few are passing me, mostly as they power along the flat. I catch up on the hills, either up or down. There are probably 10 of us riding at a similar pace but different styles, a few women, a few old men, some just out cruising. After two hours of weaving through the lower valley, we enter the beautiful and dramatic gorges before the first big hill takes us up to the high open alpine valleys and the big hill.

I can't believe it — I'm powering along, brisk pace, nothing earth-shattering of course, but all the body parts seem to be working well. In fact, I'm constantly singing, just a little ditty, 'I feel great, da de da de da, I feel great!' And I did, every turn of the pedals.

I was hydrating well, carrying the minimum in my hydration pack on my back, with two 'bidons' (water bottles to you non-cyclists) in the cages on the bike, but no fluid in them. Getting smarter in my old age, I just put the dry drink mixture in; no sense in powering that weight up hills for 50 or 60 km before drinking it now is there? As the hydration pack emptied, just before the climb up to the pass, I filled one bottle from a fast-flowing stream as I crossed it; drank it on the way up. The climb was as long as always, still people walking their bikes up though. All I can think is: 'Hey people, it's a bike, it's for riding — that's why it has wheels and pedals.'

Cresting the top, no stopping, it's all downhill from here, good tailwind too. I filled the other bidon at the bottom of the pass, enough to get me the 40-odd km home. I was flying, thanks to that helpful wind. The legs were working pretty well, full-suspension bikes were still powering past me over the ruts, but instead of anger and frustration I worked out how to nail it for next time — no movement in the ankles, in the legs at all, perhaps a light, rigid, alloy set of legs and go get a full-suspension bike: done.

The kilometres flew by; soon the smooth road that signalled the last climb was close. Hardly noticed the climb, just kept up a nice tempo and cruised up, still singing away, scaring the natives. That final downhill was a buzz, but a careful one: no sense ruining a great day by losing most of your skin to save that last couple of minutes.

The cheering crowd was exactly what I needed — I had earned it and said thanks in my mind. I wasn't any fitter before this ride compared to the previous one. Not any fitter physically that is, but fitter mentally. By having everything sorted (on all levels, daily and the future) at work, by having the right expectation of myself, I went into the epic ride in the right head space. My heart rate, my physiological performance, differed by only a few percent — the difference being that after one race I just about gave the bike away, after the other I wanted to celebrate the bike.

> ## SUMMARY PANEL
> ### The culture of the bike
>
> - *Cycling is one of the last really hard sports, in which the drive to go on and achieve must come entirely from within.*
> - *To get real performance in cycling takes a huge training commitment.*
> - *Cycling is about challenge and risk — both to your body and ego.*
> - *Cycling is a great opportunity to get more toys — great bikes are a blend of technology and art.*

20. Go high young man: what mountaineering is all about

Climbing is an instinctive thing. Just look at a child who is presented with a tree or a jungle gym. Kids spontaneously clamber up, around and over anything in their path. For them the joy of climbing is the joy of discovery, of being the highest and seeing farther than anyone else. In a lot of ways that is the joy of mountaineering for adults as well — the joy of discovery, not just of new environments and routes but of new places within yourself. It is the joy of seeing farther, both into the distance and into yourself.

Mountaineers like me seek the freedom of the hills, to experience their freedom at its exhilarating best, while at the same time appreciating that at its worst it can be discouraging, frustrating, punishing and, like many 'true sports', catastrophic.

CLIMBING: BECAUSE IT'S THERE

The problem in explaining mountaineering to others is that if they have to ask, 'Why climb?' then they probably won't understand the answer either. Ask Sir Edmund Hillary why he climbed Everest, why he crossed the Antarctic, and the answer would be the universal reply, 'Because it's there.'

I believe that understanding mountaineering, understanding the techniques and the way people climb is just another tool with which to understand life. Granted, it is not the only tool, but hopefully the information and insights from this chapter will help you appreciate the personal growth that can be achieved from passionate commitment to a discipline. So, firstly, time for a wee lesson on climbing, some descriptors and a few terms you will hear from any climber.

TYPES OF CLIMBING

Mountaineering The complete deal really, it involves all aspects of climbing. I like to think that I was a mountaineer, someone who could move through any mountain environment in the world.

Rock climbing Those gymnastic people scaling the cliffs around the country. Generally more interested in the route, in a particular line up a cliff face, than scaling a peak. 'Rock jocks' made climbing accessible to everyone, transforming the sport from the elitism of being able to access the alps, to a new elitism of technical excellence. They also introduced an aggressive new mind-set, creating the 'route' based culture we now have. They are also responsible for the imaginative naming of routes, a divergence from the typical geographical or feature naming of tradition (e.g. which sounds better, 'White Dream' or 'The central route, South Face of Aoraki'?)

Ice climbing The rock climbers of winter, climbers who seek out the merest smears of ice that form on the steepest faces, frozen waterfalls and ice-filled gullies. Traditional ice climbing has been the basis of New Zealand climbing expertise over the years (probably because our rock resembles Weet-Bix, very crumbly).

It used to involve step cutting with ice axes until technology caught up with ice climbers, who now use front point crampons and ice tools.

Sport climbing The speed version of rock climbing (sometimes ice climbing), the most obviously competitive climbing. Contestants climb a route either timed or in parallel with a competitor. Frequently practised inside on climbing walls.

Bouldering The art of climbing really technical (i.e. difficult) problems close to the ground so that when you fall, which is often, you don't need ropes or protection (although frequently a soft mat or friend is used to break the falls).

Big wall climbing Typified by the routes in America's stunning Yosemite Valley. These are rock climbs that take days — some of the early ascents took weeks — though with new techniques, equipment and training, some can now be done by the elite in a day.

Ski mountaineering Generally winter mountaineering, which apart from dealing with the intense cold of our alps in winter (generally below 0°C, and frequently -10 to -30°C), involves needing to stay above the new snow to get anywhere near some of the routes. Skis are also used to access remote wilderness areas, to ski and climb in their solitude.

Alpine style ascents When the climber carries everything they need to do a route on a mountain. It can frequently mean days of preparation getting to the start of a route, carrying extra loads, but once on the route, it is completed in one go. Traditional New Zealand and European climbing.

Expedition style ascents This is typified in Himalayan climbing, where the mountains are so big, so high and take so long, you can't carry everything in one go. Expeditions frequently use local labour (porters and guides) to help carry equipment and establish camps on the mountain. The altitude also means progress up the mountain is slow, as the climbers go high for short periods of time and then return to lower camps to recover. In essence, climbing the mountain many times before the ultimate ascent.

GEOGRAPHY FOR MOUNTAINEERS

Arête A mountain ridge, or part of one, that has the classical knife edge, almost impossible to balance on.

Bergschrund A big crevasse at the top of a slope or glacier.

Cirque The basin-shaped, steep-sided top of a valley, formed by glacial action.

Couloir A snow- and ice-filled gully.

Crevasse A deep open crack formed in the glacial ice, like a rapid in a river.

Glacier A slow-flowing river of ice, formed by the heavy snowfall high in the mountains that has compressed to ice and moves downwards by the force of gravity.

Moraine Rocks carried down by a glacier. Ice melts, rocks don't, so they gather low down on the glacier and at its end.

CLIMBING TERMS: TECHNIQUE

Belay A system used to break a fall using the climbing rope. A fixed belay is when one climber is attached to the mountain while the other is climbing. A running belay is where both climbers, roped together, climb at the same time with the rope running through protection (see below).

Belay stance An anchor position for the climber controlling the rope, ready to break the fall of the lead climber.

Cam A nifty gadget that you can insert into a crack in the rock semi-folded and the shaped sides then spread to lock it into position. Used instead of older style pitons and nuts. One cam will fit a wide range of cracks and as weight comes on it, it just locks itself in even harder — very expensive though.

Crux The most difficult section or move of a climb.

Dry tooling Using your ice tools as handholds on rock by hooking the points into cracks and notches.

Exposure There are two meanings for this word in climbing. One means hypothermia, when your body can't create enough heat for the conditions, and it can kill you. The other meaning is the feeling when there are thousands of feet of space beneath your feet: you feel exposed, like being naked in a city mall!

Freeze Like exposure, this has two meanings. Technique-wise, it means not being able to move forwards or backwards, frequently just before you fall. Mostly it is used to describe the weather conditions. 'The Freeze' is essential and occurs when the temperature drops below 0°C, allowing the snow to freeze hard. This stops lots of small rock and ice falls, and allows you to climb on the hard surface rather than sinking in.

Front pointing Climbing steep ice and snow using both ice tools and the front (toe) points of the crampons (a frame of hardened steel spikes strapped to a climber's boot). Looks and feels like freezing-cold rock climbing.

'On belay' This is called out once a climber has reached the belay stance and set up the protection to form the belay. When the other climber hears it, they know to break down their belay system and start to climb.

Pitch A section of rock, snow or ice that is climbed between belay points, ideally about the length of the rope.

Protection Any piece of equipment fixed to the rock or ice to anchor climbers or ropes to belay points. Commonly used protection includes nylon slings, snow stakes, pitons, nuts, cams and ice screws.

Soloing Climbing alone. Normally without the safety and protection of a rope, but on extreme pitches the soloist will 'self belay', setting up a belay station and placing protection to prevent too great a fall. But with no one to 'clean' the mountain afterwards, the soloist often needs to leave gear behind.

Top out or summit Finishing a climb, not necessarily at the top of a mountain.

Traverse Moving across the mountain slopes, rather than straight up.

Right, now armed with these language tools you should be able to interrogate the nearest climber to get their view on 'Why climb?' and 'How do you climb?' Be warned that climbing attracts people with a strong sense of individuality. It's rare to get exactly the same viewpoint from each.

WHY I CLIMB

The spindrift is cascading down, invading every nook and cranny, slowly filling the space between my body and the near vertical shitty ice in this hellhole of a gully. The bloody stuff is pushing me out; if I lose a foothold, if it pops my tenuous grip of two front points off, I'm in the shit. Of the two tools, the left is dry tooled over a wee lip, the right firmly planted in an ice slab that looks like it'll come away any moment. Just hang on. The only good thing is the ice crystals invading my neck — they have me shivering and shaking so much it seems to be clearing the snow away from my legs and feet.

Damn lucky I suppose that this didn't let go in 10 minutes' time. I was just taking a breather before the crux, a narrow overhanging ice spout in the neck of the gully. If I was partway through those committing moves I'd be history now. As the stream of snow and ice peters out I can think about a bit of movement. Time to check the foot placement, then hunt around for some more security for the tools. There, 20 cm away, a narrowing crack; get that left tool in there and I'll be able to hang off the sucker — the sooner the better as the isometric tension on the arms and calves is causing some pump. I can feel the lactic burn, not good with 15 metres of arm pump coming.

Lock the tool off, tie it into the harness but don't relax yet; get a cam up over to the left, get tied on, now relax. As I sit back in the harness, trying to work the tension out of arms and legs, I can see in the dull dawn the spindrift avalanche running out onto the glacial basin 500 metres below. The silence is overpowering, a dead weight on the consciousness. Time to start talking out loud to myself, feels daft and all I can think is, 'Hope no one's listening.'

'Jesus mate, what the bloody hell are you doing here by yourself? That piddly little slide could have popped you off this hill and then where would you have been, eh?'

'Right, time to keep moving, 350 metres to go yet.'

What was I doing here? Well, I guess climbers are the most dangerous of people — they dare to live their daydreams. Now normally if you get two people passionate about a sport together you end up with a bull session. Add alcohol or similar and you get dreamers that scheme. Well with climbers you only need the one dreamer. The big test for these sessions of course is what happens the next day. Does the great vision of 2 am reveal itself to be the hairy monster of your nightmares? Or does it grow with the dawn to become yet another impossible that's about to become history, another strand in the fabric of your life? Climbers turn those 2 am moments, those germs of ideas that invade your mind, into reality — and that's what I'm doing hanging here.

Time to move. The face is still in the shade but the summit ridge is catching the weak sun. Combined with the wind-loaded spindrift it will spell trouble. Time to do the Kiwi unthinkable — leave protection gear behind. How can it be, that to guarantee my life in the next 15 minutes I am worrying about leaving $250, a cam and an ice screw, behind?

'Shut up you tight arse and get on with it!'

The trick when soloing is knowing your ultimate limit, when to protect yourself, and I'm feeling particularly chicken at the moment. So time to rope up. Ten minutes to set up, some movement giving me a bit of confidence and much-needed warmth back. Small spindrift showers stream over like a silken stream, with the odd 'whizz' of small ice blocks or rocks further out.

With the self belay set up — no more excuses — I reach out, up high to the right, and plant a tool. Step across to a small toe ledge, crampons scraping unstably, bit of a bounce to check and commitment time. Swing out, and start the chess-like moves, 'think man, think', every breath, every placement has to be right and fast. I don't have the excess strength to hang around.

Up the vertical messy ice smear and sink the tools into the hopefully solid overhanging ice bulge; the next three metres are critical. Must move fast and positive, an almost dynamic continuous flow of moves. Up over the bulging ice, the front points on the left foot let go, breaking clear of the ice, foot swinging free, along with my heart (it feels as if it's going a million beats per second). With the crampon points scrabbling for purchase, they find just enough to bite to push me up and clear the overhang — the 90-degree gully above feeling like a football field compared with the dark, claustrophobic hole below.

I move quickly over to the side, only a couple of moves but out of the direct line of fire from the ice and rocks falling from above. Haul the rope up; should I use it for this next pitch? Probably should, but bugger it, it'll take too long. Surplus gear packed and it's on up the left edge of the gully, still 80 degrees, steep, but OK ice, plenty of points in, feeling pretty stable. The gully peters out to the broad ice cap and even though it's only 70 degrees the feeling of exposure is huge, really making you concentrate every second.

I don't look down, 1500 metres to the glacier below is too far. Turn around and it just wants to pull you off. The urge to hug the ice (and risk falling as the angles of contact for the crampons is all wrong) is almost as great as the urge to step out into the void. The air feels cold and dense, as though it would cushion your flight down. Lack of food and too much adrenaline, just need to keep it together for another 100 metres; repetitive front pointing, just the time to make a mistake, not. The wind is picking up, starting to buffet my pack, just has to hold off another hour.

Bugger going to the top, I skirt around the ice cap trying to keep out of the full blast of the wind, occasionally peeking over the ridge at evil-looking steely grey wisps of cloud. How the hell do I get off this pig of a hill? Lack of sugar is slowing the brain but nowhere to stop; my drink tube has frozen so no help there, just keep on going.

Hour after hour, picking my way down the shattered rock and patchy ice of the ridge, sidling around small unstable towers, downclimbing the heads of gullies and traversing sharp ridges, all the while keeping out of the killer wind. The bergschrund gave some respite, time to eat a couple of bars, slurp some partially frozen drink. Once over this it's just careful weaving and I'm home free — near enough anyway.

Two choices. Jump, one metre out, four metres down onto a steep slope, but — what's it like? Hard? Soft? Will it avo? Too many decisions.

Or sacrifice a snow stake and rap down? The slope below is as hard as glass, damn lucky I didn't jump, I'd be a human missile if I had.

Back to downclimbing, front pointing backwards, constantly looking over my shoulder, the pack getting heavier and heavier. Dumb arse; I stand up. As I've been downclimbing the slope has almost flattened. Twenty minutes later I flop down outside the bivvy shelter, just a corrugated iron hovel really, no bunks, nothing but shelter from that annoying wind.

Brew time, sleep time. The wind is causing those old nightmares again, of being blown off mountains, like being hit by a freight train. I drift off to an uneasy sleep, but wake to complete silence; it feels like sacrilege to make the slightest sound, the creaking of the tin door offensive in the dawn.

This is why I climb. Sitting in the bitterly cold dawn, fresh powder dusting the peaks that tower above, looking as though they are leaning in to touch each other over my head. Laid out above is the wall, the narrow, twisting, almost vertical, frequently overhanging smear of ice that I had climbed — yep me, I had done that. No one will ever take that away. I have that for life, another tick in the book. I seriously frightened myself yesterday, more than once, and I am a stronger being for it — that's why I climb.

> **SUMMARY PANEL**
> **Go high young man**
>
> - *Climbing is the 'must do' concept in practice.*
> - *Every mountain is like a mirror, it reveals and reflects your character.*
> - *People climb for many different reasons but the love of the mountains and the intimate experience they provide underpins them all.*

21. You are what you eat

Food is the cornerstone of life. Its presence is essential to keep the exquisitely designed engines that are our bodies operating, but even more importantly it's a source of inspiration and enjoyment for many of us. However, just like wine, food attracts so much bullshit — everyone is an expert. So many people have an opinion or a 'barrow to push' that often the facts get mislaid. While I don't want to preach I would like to promote a few basic facts and the science behind them.

NO MAGIC BULLET

Nutrition is one of those areas in life where everyone looks for the 'magic bullet'. Well, despite what heaps of people might tell you otherwise, it doesn't exist at present (though don't worry, I'm sure still looking).

Nutrition (and my apologies to all those experts out there for simplifying it) is all about balance and timing. Balance, because for most of us (excluding medical conditions) weight is the most pressing issue we have. Simply because the energy that goes in as food is more than we expend during the day. So how do we manage that? Well that's balance as well: up the activity, the energy expenditure and put in the appropriate amount.

Timing is also important, especially if you want to include exercise in your life, and essential if you want to be an athlete. While *what* we eat for life and health is critical, *when* we eat it determines the efficiency and subsequent performance we extract from our bodies.

'Diets' are simply what we do by eating every day. The extreme sort are frequently physiologically incorrect, can do you serious damage, and are what many of the 'fad' diet people want you to use.

There is a lot of good advice out there, and some of the respected commercial companies offer a managed, and far more complete, version of the suggestions I offer here. While I don't have specific dietary qualifications I do have some experiences that may interest you.

THE INGLIS 'DIET'

Take a very cold room — let's say -10° — and make yourself as comfortable as possible. Wear some three layers of clothing: woollen underwear, pile jumper and Gore-Tex jacket and pants. Now you are set up to expend about 24,000 kilojoules (or for those as old as me, about 6000 calories). The Inglis diet then calls for about one Shrewsbury biscuit per day, a few spoonfuls of drink concentrate, a small slice of canned peach and half a cup of water. That all amounts to, in technical terms, not much.

That's the diet that Phil Doole and I subsisted on in Middle Peak Hotel for the first 160 hours, over six days. After 310 hours, nearly 13 days (even though some more substantial food had been air-dropped in), I had lost a third of my body weight. It wasn't just body fat I lost either, as I didn't have a lot to begin with. I lost a significant amount of muscle mass as well. I also came close to losing my life through malnutrition, with its associated kidney and liver damage — a rather dramatic diet.

OK, so I know what diet not to do. Because let's face it, it is no use being skinny and unhealthy. The whole essence of food and life has to be health. Be it sport, business, or just the mundane process of living life, without health everything is so much harder.

By the time I graduated from Lincoln University in 1989 I had spent a significant proportion of my time learning about nutrition. I studied under Dr Geoff Savage, a leading expert in the metabolism of amino acids (the building blocks of our bodies), leading eventually to my first-class honours degree in biochemistry. With its complex interactions between so many sciences, I loved biochemistry with a passion. Through it I discovered many of the mysteries of life, how the internals of our ultimate engine work and relate to each other. In fact, it is the basis of numerous professions, such as winemaking, nutrition, medicine, brewing, cooking, and all life in general really.

BASICS OF NUTRITION
Let's cover a few facts first:

Aerobic exercise
This means 'with oxygen'. It's the main system our bodies use to power us through the day.

Anaerobic exercise
This means 'without oxygen', really high effort work. We can't sustain getting our power this way for long. It acts a bit like a car turbo or nitrous boost.

Carbohydrate
This is the high octane fuel for everyone, by far the most efficient and the most effective fuel for aerobic exercise, also the main recharger of our batteries. Carbohydrate ('carbs') is essentially sugars in their many forms, of which the simplest and easiest used is glucose. Our bodies' biochemistry is tailored to turn carbohydrates into glucose which is then stored as glycogen in the liver and muscles. It is glycogen that our

muscles recruit to power them, sourcing it from both those muscle and liver stores. In an average balanced diet we should be getting about 60 percent of our energy intake from carbs, higher for endurance athletes. If you eat too much carbohydrate for the storage room available as glycogen then it goes straight to fat.

Protein

Proteins are the building blocks of our bodies, they form our muscles and are built out of amino acids. The whole basis of our genetic make-up, DNA, is to create a code to manufacture and order our amino acids, hence building the individual proteins that make up our bodies.

Proteins can be used for energy but they are far more important in rebuilding the damage we do ourselves as we train and live life. If your glycogen levels are low before exercise (because you didn't eat enough carbohydrate at the right time) then you will use at least twice as much protein for energy than otherwise (10 percent compared to four percent on average), which is a very inefficient source of energy and often damaging to your body. The reality is that most people (except vegans and a few other unique dieters) eat far more protein than they will ever need.

Fat

The big 'boogie man' of any diet but an essential element nonetheless. The trouble is, like protein, we tend to eat far too much, and even worse, the wrong types of fat. Apart from many fats being chock-full of cholesterol (another essential for life, but when overindulged in will kill you), fat is an important energy source for low-level aerobic activity, especially endurance events.

We all have a similar storage capacity for carbohydrates, but vary greatly in our fat stores — in fact, at the moment I think mine could let me do far more than just the 13 days I managed in Middle Peak Hotel in 1982! When we eat more than we need, or the wrong balance of foods, then it goes straight to fat — pretty simple really.

Fat takes a long time to be utilised, both being stored and subsequently when being used. It also has more energy per gram than any other food (38 kJ or nine calories per gram compared to carbs and protein at 17 kJ or four calories per gram). While too much fat will kill you (via various forms of heart disease and related disorders), no fat or very low fat diets can also eventually kill you as many of our vitamins and essential fatty acids (both essential for healthy cell structure and function) are carried in the fat we eat.

Water

Yep, water is just as important a nutrient as carbohydrates, proteins and fats. No matter what you are doing, a small level of dehydration will adversely affect your performance. Even a two percent decrease in body fluid will decrease exercise potential by at least 10 percent, not to mention slow your thinking and make all the functions of your body work much harder.

Always keep water around, not fizzy drinks or juice, but plain old water. It's not calories you need from it during the day (though that works as well, as long as you remove the same number of calories from somewhere else) but cooling and lubrication. I'm sure we have all seen the extremes of dehydration — such as the unfortunate Craig Barrett in the 50-km walk at the Kuala Lumpur Commonwealth Games and images of people lost in the Australian outback — but almost every day we suffer mild dehydration, especially working in air-conditioned environments. In most hotels, I'll drink 600 ml overnight and will still be dehydrated in the morning (yes, OK, I'll drink a litre from now on).

It's easy to tell when you are hydrated — your urine will be clear. If it's not then either you need to drink more or you are taking a substance that colours your pee (don't laugh, many vitamin tablets will do this, which is very confusing if you are trying to gauge your hydration level).

Vitamins and minerals

Apart from some medical conditions, if you are eating that balanced diet then it's rare that you need a vitamin boost. Vitamins are essential compounds that our bodies don't make, so we have to get them or their precursors in our diet. The ones to really watch are calcium, iron, folate, vitamin B6, B12 and riboflavin. Don't fall into the trap of 'if a little is good, more is better', because with vitamins the opposite is generally true. Vitamins can be classed as either fat or water soluble. Overindulge in water soluble and you'll just pee it out generally (like vitamin C), but overindulge in fat soluble ones and they will accumulate in your tissues, especially the liver, and do you great harm.

KEEP A FOOD DIARY

To work out just how you eat and what you eat it is really valuable to do a food diary. It doesn't have to be elaborate, just keep a notebook and honestly write down what and how much you have every time you eat or drink something — no cheating though. Most of us get quite a surprise and can learn heaps about what we need to change. The most common things that a food diary highlights are:

- A lack of good fluids, that is just plain water or low-sugar fruit or sports drinks
- Too many refined sugars, generally from soda-style drinks and sweet foods
- An excess of protein
- A lack of fresh fruit and vegetables
- Just how many calories alcoholic drinks contribute to a diet.

My advice isn't just for dieters and athletes — some of the worst nutritional practices I have seen belong to businesspeople.

TRAVELLING

Eating appropriately and well while travelling is difficult and sometimes boring. The secret? Well, I travel a lot, and I find that for me the best strategy is to utilise services such as airline club lounges (such as Koru Club), where you can relax, do some work and build a healthy tasty snack yourself. Carry fruit, but not into New Zealand, healthy fruit-based snack bars and plenty of water. Go easy on the coffee though, it dehydrates you, and if you are a caffeine addict you will need more and more each day to get the same kick as time goes on. Going out to dinner every night is just as boring and tiring as never going out, and what makes it more difficult is that you can't control what goes into that stunning dish in front of you. Try eating two entrées instead of an entrée and a main — you'll get a better variety of food without ending up like a blimp and you may even have room for a dessert.

RULES FOR REFUELLING

You may have guessed already that to maintain a healthy diet we don't need to be 'food Nazis', but simply eat a wide range of foods from that simple food pyramid we should all be familiar with.

Here are some straightforward rules to live and train by when refuelling:

- Choose a wide variety of foods from all the major food groups; as I said, there is no one magic bullet.
- Eat enough carbohydrate for your activity level and body size, especially complex food such as vegetables and grains.
- Avoid 'fad' diets, keep body weight reasonable through balanced foods and exercise.
- Back off on the fat and protein, almost invariably we eat too much of both.
- Water is our coolant, drink plenty (the body can clear about 600–800 ml per hour) all day and at night. If you don't get up to pee at night you probably haven't drunk enough (excluding problems with the ageing waterworks of course). Yes you can drink too much — hyperhydration is when you drink more than you can clear, and the sodium and other minerals in your bloodstream become diluted producing symptoms such as

- vomiting and dizziness.
- Missing meals means the body becomes more efficient at using and storing food — more small meals are a far better strategy for everyone.
- Ensure you get enough calcium and iron in your diet.
- Do a big breakfast, but not one chock-full of fat. Try a bowl of cereal, some toast and lots of fruit, and back it up with a big glass of water and some fruit juice.
- Refuel with carbohydrates straight after training: fruit juice, rice, breads, whatever takes your fancy (because food has to taste good), but it is very important to do it within 20 minutes of finishing so that you will train better the next day. Don't do it and you'll have heavy tired limbs the next day — another day wasted.
- Keep a food diary for seven days and look at it critically (we are very good at fooling ourselves), or even better, spend a few dollars and take it along to a dietician or nutritionist.
- Most importantly, learn to cook great food — one of the greatest skills you can have for an interesting life.

Feel free to listen to the advice of others (and that includes my advice as well) but please take that advice to a registered nutritionist or doctor before committing yourself and your body to a specific regime.

SUMMARY PANEL
You are what you eat

- *Drink plenty.*
- *There is no magic bullet other than good balanced nutrition.*
- *Be aware of what you eat and drink — you control it, no excuses.*
- *Spend some time learning about food and its components.*
- *If what you eat doesn't taste good, it makes for a very boring life.*

Summary

22. Tying it all together: lifelong learning

So many of the lessons about life that I have learned over the years can be used not just in sports such as mountaineering and cycling, or in businesses like the wine industry, but in every facet of our lives. Much of what I have written about here I class as 'learning for life, lifelong learning'. The Japanese culture expresses it as *kaizen*, which can essentially be expressed as 'the spirit of continuous improvement'. Too often we hear the axiom, 'If it ain't broke, don't fix it'. Hear that too often, or even worse, believe it, and all innovation and growth, whether business or personal, will stop.

Evaluation of what has been and evaluation of current performance is critical to growth. It is both the first and last step of learning from living.

Ideally, what you will have gained from the life lessons presented in this book can be visualised like this:

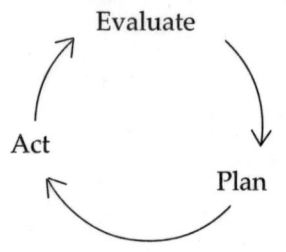

```
        Evaluate
       ↗        ↘
    Act          ↓
       ↖        
         Plan
```

This is a continuous loop — in which evaluation is both the first and last step — to help you grow.

Likewise, I believe there are four critical requirements for any organisation or team to achieve excellence, to operate effectively in that loop, and they are:

1. Enough people and resources on the team to complete the essential tasks for maintenance and growth (plan, plan and plan again).
2. Each of those team members is fully informed (shares the dream).
3. The team can interact freely and each member has the skills of effective communication relevant to their position.
4. The culture of the team leads to an environment of trust — win-win must be at the core of all interactions.

When each of these four criteria is satisfied then the individual and the team are in a position to grow, are primed to transform that dream into reality.

As an individual, to create an optimistic outlook is essential for that healthy life. If you can practise even some of the habits below every day then you'll be just that bit further ahead:

- To be strong so nothing will disturb your peace of mind.
- To talk health, happiness and prosperity to all.

- To make your friends feel there is something in them.
- To look on the sunny side, make your optimism come true.
- To think and expect only the best.
- To be as enthusiastic about the success of others as about your own successes.
- To learn from the achievements and mistakes of the past to create the greater achievements of the future.
- To be so busy striving for your own improvement you have no time to criticise others.
- To be too large for worry, too noble for anger, too strong for fear, and too happy to permit the presence of trouble.

For me the core of life is challenge. I passionately believe that we all need some sort of risk to develop; it's like the power to the pedals of our life cycle.

We owe it to ourselves to dream big, but to always do it with passion and commitment.

There are no stumbling blocks in life, just stepping stones; there are no impossibles, just possibles not yet achieved; there are no problems, just new and different opportunities.

Mark Inglis
May 2003
www.markinglis.co.nz
www.middlepeak.co.nz

MARK INGLIS

NO MEAN FEAT

Many New Zealanders will remember November 1982, when Mark Inglis was trapped with fellow climber, Phil Doole, for 13 days in an ice cave near the summit of Mount Cook. They survived through raging blizzards, with minimal equipment and very little food. By the time they were air-lifted from the mountain both men had severe frostbite and had to have their legs amputated below the knee.

Since that time Mark has transformed his life. He has been a research scientist and has made medal-winning wines with Montana. He has won a silver medal cycling at the Sydney 2000 Paralympic Games, and, in 2002, to his great joy, he stepped onto the summit of Mount Cook again.

This is an inspiring story of remarkable courage and determination. For Mark Inglis, challenge in life is paramount and every new adventure brings with it the opportunity to live life to its fullest.

For Mark Inglis, life is for living and obstacles are there to be overcome. Every new adventure brings with it new challenges and the opportunity to live life TO THE MAX.

TO THE MAX is the teen reader's version of NO MEAN FEAT.